INSIDE
THE PAIN

A SURVIVOR'S GUIDE TO BREAKING THE CYCLES
OF ABUSE AND DOMESTIC VIOLENCE

BRENDA FIREEAGLE BIDDIX

Written by: Brenda (FireEagle) Biddix

This is for all the lonely, hurting, and confused people. And for the victims who inspired this work by overcoming their suffering.

Thanks to all the friends and family who have stood by me throughout this project.

Introduction

This book is based on the stories of five courageous women. Each of them have survived and overcome the harrowing experience of domestic violence. I am one of them. Our journeys are testimonies of resilience, strength, and the unyielding human spirit.

Why are so many women hurting today?

We live in a world where the pressures on women are immense. Single mothers, busy professionals, and those struggling with mental health issues often ask: **Can I heal? Are long-term relationships achievable?** Modern women endure emotional turmoil, including depression and anxiety. Societal pressures to balance relationships, careers, and motherhood add to this stress.

The societal expectations placed upon women are daunting and often unrealistic. This leads to a myriad of disorders affecting their well-being. Today, women must excel at work, be perfect mothers, maintain relationships, and continue their education. They must do this while managing their mental health. The intersection of these roles can create an overwhelming sense of pressure and inadequacy.

Can we heal? Yes, we can. This book, through the stories of five women, aims to illuminate the path to healing and recovery. We delve into the struggles, the pain, and ultimately, the triumphs. Our stories are not just about survival. They are about thriving despite the odds.

This book is a beacon of hope for women who feel trapped in the cycle of abuse and despair. It is a reminder that while the journey to healing is arduous, it is possible. By sharing our experiences, we hope to inspire others to seek help, find their strength, and reclaim their lives. Together, we can end the silence and stigma around domestic violence. The vision of this book is to create a future where all women can live free from fear and pain. We just need to learn how.

The Effect of Domestic Violence

Domestic violence impacts victims physically, psychologically, socially, and economically. This issue affects not only adults but also their children. Resources like "Inside the Pain" offer hope and healing.

Expert Testimonials

"*Inside the Pain* is a crucial resource for those affected by domestic violence, offering hope and practical steps for healing."
— Mark Cadavero, MSW, LCSW, Clinical Director, Murphy Counseling Services

"This book is especially needed among Latina women. A Spanish edition would greatly benefit the Latina Women's Support Group."
— Rosario Villarrael, Founder, "Follow Your Dream: Resources to Start Your Own Business"

"*Inside The Pain* is not just a book~ it's a lifeline. A must read for all women!"
— Nadeanne Kleinman, Ph.D., Clinical Psychologist

Author's Thoughts:

I believe that seeking solutions is better than allowing this to persist. Abuse has gone on for centuries. It's been both physical and emotional. It will be hard to address, but we can do it. Solutions do exist…

About the Author

Brenda FireEagle Biddix was born in the Southern Appalachian Mountains in 1950. She studied creative writing, psychiatric nursing, and clinical nursing. These fields gave her deep insights into human resilience and spirit, which greatly influenced her writing.

A dedicated mother and advocate, Brenda has mentored youth and fought domestic violence in her church and community. Her literary works have been featured in *Lamplighter Magazine, Guns and Ammo*, and various newspapers.

She has received the Editor's Choice Award and was nominated for Poet of the Year by the International Symposium of Poets. Despite having Parkinson's, her creativity has thrived. She wrote "Pond Water" and its sequel, "Pond Water Riptide" which have gone viral on TikTok.

This book is a testament to Brenda's unwavering spirit and resilience.

Brenda hopes this book provides the strength and guidance you need to navigate any challenges you face. Your support makes a significant difference in her life. All proceeds from this book go towards helping her with her medical bills and other challenges. Thank you for going on this journey and celebrating her incredible legacy.

PART I

Recognizing Who You Are

First of all, women should remember that they are somebody. They are somebody simply because they exist. A woman's worth is not determined by the man at her side. It is not set by her education, job, paycheck, home, neighborhood, color, or origin. It is determined by what she thinks of herself.

Many women fail to recognize hurtful remarks for what they truly are. These are not the words of a man who cherishes her "as his own body, feeding and nourishing it." Rather, they are cruel, calculating remarks meant to control her. Anyone who believes they must control another does so because they are insecure. There is nothing a woman can do to help someone like that, especially by being their doormat. Such a person would never admit they had a problem. Anything that goes wrong will usually be someone else's fault. It's often their mate's, but never their own. A woman will only reap greater frustration and grief if she tries to change such a person. Marriage vows do not bind a woman to a controlling mate. To such a man, they are like a title deed to a car, a house, or a pet. With that piece of paper, he sees himself as gaining ownership of his mate's person. She cannot alter his opinion or his way of thinking. She needs to work on herself. That's not to say he will never accept responsibility for his choices. Each person is responsible for their own choices. In today's world, marriage is a revolving door, rarely seen as sacred. When a man sees a woman working on herself, he may see the need for his own change. But it is far more likely he will feel threatened. A woman can reassure her mate. She can say that she is improving for both of them and for their relationship. Again, his growth should not become her objective. It is reasonable to add that there is one other possibility. His insecurity and abuse may get worse. At this juncture, a woman must take measures for her own safety and that of any children. She must not give up on herself. She must ask herself, "Do I want to have a happy, fulfilling life for myself and my children?"

Now, it should be asked, "Do you have an example in your life to study? Do you know what to strive for?" Alice Von Hildebrand, PhD, called the movement "catastrophic feminism." But has all the effort and anger really freed anyone? It may be true that some good laws have come from the decades of conflict. For example, laws on equal pay and time off for childbirth. Many employers now provide childcare facilities. However, what about the negative effects? "What is driving kids today?" There is a breakdown in the family unit and the absence of moral values. Alice found a starting point for us to rebuild our families today within religious texts. I hope you allow me to use the word God in this book. Even if you haven't considered it before, God was a solid foundation that I was able to turn to as well. Having a sanctuary beyond home laid the foundation that made recovery possible.

Let's get personal. People in church can turn away from us. I had bruises on me, and believers told me I should have been obedient. So, when I say to turn to

God for answers, it comes from a place of being hurt myself. I want to help you out of this, in the way that worked for me. A woman who is agnostic or atheistic has a greater battle. The chance of change will be harder. She has to figure out all the things that religious texts can teach her.

"Keep your chin up."

"Just hang in there."

"You have to get tough."

"You're just overreacting." You've heard all the well-meaning remarks, good, bad, or indifferent. Are the people who are telling you these things really your friends? Or are they just in the same kind of mess and don't have any hope either? Are they friends like many have had, trying to find a way to accuse you and justify their own suffering? Don't fall into the trap of false humility either. Humility is great! But self-deprecation is not humility. Humility is being who you really are, not what someone else wants you to be.

A person can become desensitized. They get numb to their circumstances and start thinking irrationally. There is an old saying that compares a painful relationship to an old pair of shoes. The shoes are worn, run over, and the nails are poking through. They hurt, but you keep wearing them. After all, at least you know where the nails are. A new pair may be too tight or too loose or... In the same way, women are often afraid of change. An abusive, subservient life is, at least, familiar. We learn what to expect, perhaps just as we saw Mom. We know when to cower, duck, or have dinner on the table, a 'cold one' in hand. That may be all you've ever known but that does not make it right. So why do we continue to accept it? Apathy? Lack of feeling or emotion leads to disaster. It may seem so. But, remember, 'You Are Somebody.' Through the talks I've had with other survivors, it becomes apparent that we are all alike. Not a servant, a sex object, a possession, a punching bag, etc.

Who are you? You may not even have a clue. Let's see, ummm? So-and-so's girlfriend, old lady, Dick and Jane's Mom? Your job? Or, how about a really common answer? I'm nobody. No, no, no! Take a deep breath. Exhale. Close your eyes for a second, then we'll go on. There is no great mystery here. It doesn't matter your ethnicity or religion. Most American women agree: they will readily say that God made men and women. God himself declared, approving his creation, calling it "very good." Both Christian and non-Christian persuasions perceive there to be a creator-God. So, if the Maker puts his seal of approval on you, why can't you? Shall we go a step further? You are his child, whom he wants to bless and whom he loves. It is not the purpose of this work to sound sanctimonious. Nor to imply that any of us have it all together. Far from it. Anyone who has ever been in our position would find it hard to ever think of us in such a way.

It is just as hard to see ourselves as a child of God while we remain in our situation. To achieve this requires real effort. Relating personal horror stories would be of no benefit. Each of us has our own tale, and what would be a horror story to one may pass easily for another day. The key, of course, is to learn who we are, why we make certain kinds of choices, and what we can do to change them. Try saying, "I'm a mess. But I'm God's mess, and he loves me, just as I am, faults and all!" Come on. It isn't meant to make you feel silly. You are, you know, original, and being one of a kind is a beautiful thing. Most of us can mark places in our lives by when 'we were in charge' of our lives. At the opposite end of our spectrum are the times when God was allowed to be in control. There are far fewer of those times. It could be summed up: "If I have my hands on the controls, whatever the situation, it failed. This happens sooner rather than later. I could mess up a one-car parade. Lay out the route and I'd get turned around." Ego and self-confidence are two different emotions, with very different motives. Reaching the point of accepting the difference doesn't happen instantly. You have to truly recognize it. Nor does reaching the point of accepting and confessing our blundering, inept choices. Changing your opinion of yourself takes real work. Admitting your faults does not mean a woman needs to punish herself. Besides, cat-o-nine-tails aren't too common these days.

Learn to laugh at your ineptitude, screw-ups; try not to repeat them. The painful part is being honest with yourself. Accept responsibility for your own life, including the choices you've made. "Poor, pitiful me," and similar ideas will get you nowhere. Honesty, albeit uncomfortable, is the only way to proceed. The friend who told you to "get tough" was closest to being right; although, she probably had no concept of the half of it.

Becoming a whole woman and ending the cycle of pain and failure can never be realized by a perpetual victim. We create the world we live in by the choices we make. My physical and emotional pain didn't last forever. You only have to take the power back from it. We cannot blame our parents, caregivers, partners, or fate for our lives. These words can influence our self-esteem. Hearing "you're stupid" or "you can be anything you choose" can stick with us. But words alone can't create change. We can tell ourselves to remember to do things and still forget. Likewise, people can tell us things about ourselves that aren't accurate. Peers or parents will find a way to ridicule you, but that doesn't mean you have to believe them. However, if prolonged, it may have the appearance of being the normal way to live. When a woman gets used to an abusive lifestyle, it's hard to see that the change must come. Those who are in pain look to get out of being in pain. An abuser, unfortunately, may feel stronger by putting others down. So real change can only begin with the ones who are abused.

The despair, the bleakness of the environment lends no hope, no ray of light. As women, we tend to believe that by some miracle or magic, men will become our vision of Prince Charming. He will come into our lives and rescue us from all the problems in our lives. We fail to see our misguided judgment. We attract, not Prince Charming, but the kind of people who now surround us. Is there any hope? What can we do? Human answers and logic defy our reason. Why? How? What? Often, it would seem there are no answers. None you can find.

You are looking in every direction, from the bottom of a really dark hole, and you can't see how you can ever get out. Looking up, the top seems so very far away.

Many women spend countless dollars on counseling and motivational seminars. These can cost a lot and have limited success. We must each decide to change ourselves to end the misery. Women are in a web of abuse, anxiety, depression, and failure. They become too afraid to trust anyone or believe anything they hear. What a mess!

Dr. Bernie Seagal faced a crisis. After some study, he turned his crisis into a way of helping others. He was curious about the power of *love* taught in religion. Through years of study, he discovered this. Within religion, the goal was to help others recover. His discoveries also helped his clients face terminal illnesses with greater success. Our openness and attitude affect our lives. Life is a labor pain, according to Dr. Seagal. Joy is born from our choices over time. When you have arthritis, it is painful to move, but the movement helps the body manage the arthritis. Some may think that studying God to improve our lives would be painful. But it helps us make better decisions.

When we identify the sources of our pain, we can allow it to teach and direct us. We cannot merely say someone makes our life "a living hell." We have to ask, why does this person make our existence so unbearable?

We can use Dr. Seagal again as an example. He did not let his ordeal defeat him. Instead of being overwhelmed by his challenges, he sought God to gain clarity in his life. He used the art of archery to explain his life. Dr. Seagal painted a vivid picture of not knowing where or how to aim. What were we shooting for? Why was the pain not going away? We have our bow, our arrows, and our target. "There are many targets out there," stated Dr. Seagal. "It's about aiming your arrow at the right target. Those in pain are like archers, full of arrows. All the energy going to the wrong places.

Putting our spouses in the line of fire is missing the mark. Our lives will reflect where we've directed our arrows. We can use them to improve our lives and also tear them down. There's a wide area on the target, but we need archery training to hit the right mark."

It is essential for a woman to examine where she stands. She is preparing herself as a heavenly bride. If she doesn't feel the love, peace, joy, and abundant life she deserves, where should she start? Simply praying for change would be ineffective. That would be like handing God a long shopping list and saying, "I need/want all these things. You sort it out. I want..., I want..., I want..." What do you need?

A woman, whether she is a Christian or not, needs to understand herself and know where to go. We can set aside social and religious boundaries for this point. The choices she has made have brought her to her current situation. To repent is to feel sorry, to be willing to modify the situation, and to be stricken in conscience. Success requires a willingness to face personal shortcomings, readiness to adapt, and total honesty. Does it sound hard? Even impossible? Hard, yes. But impossible, no.

The transition is not about hammering yourself mentally or verbally. Ruminating only keeps our pain fresh and becomes a repeated target. You have endured enough of that kind of treatment. Be honest, but kind to yourself. Within honesty, you will find the avenue to understanding how you have arrived at where you are today. Being anything but truly candid with yourself would be no less than lying to yourself.

Are you ready to begin a journey of discovery? Your own epic saga of life? Using the following questions as a guideline, form direct questions to fit your life. It cannot be stressed enough to be truthful with your answers. Don't rush. No one but you needs to ever see your work. There are no wrong answers. It is not a graded test nor a timed quiz. Your every answer is important and correct, as long as it is truthful. Proceed to the next question only after you have fully assessed the current one to the best of your ability.

Self-Exam

Question 1. Are you happy with your life right now? Take a moment to study these questions...

- This question helps us reflect on our current state, making us aware of the underlying stresses. Without admitting or realizing there's a problem, things won't get better.

Question 2. What do you really want out of life? What do you want it to look like?

- By identifying your dreams, you give yourself a chance to live them.

Question 3. Is there something missing in your life? What do you long for that nothing seems to satisfy?

- This question encourages us to pinpoint any feelings of emptiness, which the book can address.

Question 4. Do you often feel stuck or trapped? What makes you feel that way?

- Understanding feelings of being stuck helps us recognize what is causing our anxiety.

Question 5. What choices have you made that got you here?

- Reflecting on past choices allows us to take ownership of our journey and prepares us for a better future.

Question 6. Why did you make those choices? What were you hoping for?

- This question helps us understand our motivations and patterns. If we don't know we are making mistakes, we keep repeating them.

Question 7. Are you struggling with depression, anxiety, anger, fear, or feeling controlled by sex?

- Identifying our specific struggles opens the door to discussing solutions that will work for us.

Question 8. What worries you the most right now?

- Addressing current worries can help us find immediate relief.

Question 9. Do you feel overwhelmed or exhausted by life? Are there ways to improve this?

- Understanding sources of exhaustion can lead us to explore ways to lighten the load or even improve how we feel day-to-day.

Question 10. Who do you spend the most time with? How do they influence you?

- Reflecting on relationships helps us see the impact of those around us on our well-being.

Question 11. What's most important to you in life? What do you spend most of your time and energy on?

- This question aligns us with our core values and highlights potential misalignments.

Question 12. What's the one thing you want to achieve more than anything else? Why is it so important to you?

- Focusing on a primary goal can motivate us and give us a sense of purpose.

As you ponder these questions, you might start to see patterns and areas in your life that need attention. This self-examination is just the beginning of your journey. Throughout this book, we will explore these feelings and challenges in greater depth. We'll talk about practical steps to help you reclaim your life, find fulfillment, and embrace your true potential. You are not alone. Together, we will find the path to healing and self-discovery.

Reflecting on my own experiences, I remember things I haven't thought about in years. But I am here for you. We are in this darkness together, and I have brought my lantern to help us find our way out.

Forming these or similar questions will aid a woman in assessing her plight more clearly. If the picture seems bleak, now is NOT the time to quit. Overall and all at once, the problems will seem insurmountable. Working through each one individually is less daunting. Admitting unhappiness is easy, and listing the reasons is simple. But what about the choices? Oh, yes. CHOICES! We tend to wince at those. They are the only part of our plight that we are responsible for.

By looking at a few scenarios, we can discern how a woman might find herself in a difficult situation. In the first scenario, imagine you were always seen as a good girl. After high school, you got your first job, an apartment, and a boyfriend who talks about marriage. You were considering college but decided to take the summer to make a final decision. Now, you find out you're pregnant!

Synopsis: Seeing yourself as an adult woman, you leapt into adult decision-making. Too quickly? Examine each step you've made, accepting responsibility for YOUR choices. Closer scrutiny will show something. You were drawn to a perfect relationship. This led you to give in to the partnership that caused the pregnancy. You thought the man would be overjoyed. You told him you were going to bear his child and move forward with the marriage plans. But, he is acting like a jerk and wants you to have an abortion. He cuts you to the heart, adding that he thinks you both should see other people.

SLAP! Not physically, but verbally. He even now denies being the father. What do you do? He's willing to pay for an abortion. You decide to keep your child. You love it, and you loved him. You thought you knew him, right? Next, you learn he's done this before and won't offer support.

An analogy can be drawn from a card game. Life deals us cards, but it is us who decide which ones we play. Rather than self-pity, "Why me, Lord?" ask that same Lord, "How would you have me handle this?" Your next decision is what is key now. Will you rise above your mistakes and go on? Or, will you fall for the next guy who comes along promising you the moon but can't deliver a free meal? Too frequently, women move in with the next guy or allow him to move in with her. She is vulnerable, afraid she can't make it on her own. She fears making more bad choices. She doubts her ability to choose. The hormones in her body make this fear worse. She feels undesirable, unlovable, stupid, and even fat. A man showing interest in her gives her a false sense of security. It leads her to explain away any problems as "just my condition." She craves love and acceptance. All moral lessons she has learned are out the window. Why?

Stepping back for a moment, when did her decisions go awry? She had a job, albeit cashiering in fast food, etc. It gave her a feeling of independence and maturity. Was she as mature as she thought? Was she really ready to move out on her own? Or, did she just want to be grown up? Was the boyfriend someone she had known for a long time? How well did they know each other? Were the choices made in love, or was lust the driving factor? Love is more than sex. It doesn't seek its own gratification, nor does it behave obscenely.

So, were decisions to have intercourse made in love or lust? She found that some mistakes caused her problem. Will she make it worse with more mistakes? It is unfortunate that most women do just that. Why is it so hard for a woman to see that the same girl who attracted her lost love is even more radiant as a mother? She fails to realize she is easy prey for unscrupulous men who see an easy time with a woman in an unwed pregnancy. He doesn't need to take precautions against getting you pregnant. And if you think he'll be thinking about giving you an STD or getting any, you're wrong. Once your child is born, reality sets in. The flaws and problems you thought were due to pregnancy and would go away are not gone. More times than not, the differences only worsen. The man in the picture is usually very controlling. You are no longer so dependent upon all his attention. You have a tiny person dependent on you. Now you're not pregnant. You're less dependent and assert yourself more. He sees this as a threat to his position. He becomes more controlling. He needs you to be dependent upon him to feel secure. Confrontation brings out the worst in both parties, leading to a breakup or abuse. Sadly, more children may be born and drawn into the situation. Even more pregnancies may happen if the situation goes on. Until a concerted effort is made individually to create change, the pattern repeats.

If you entered into the relationship unhappy, you'll both be unhappy. Married or single, a woman must search herself for the answers. It isn't God who has given up on you. He doesn't do recalls for defects or potential risks. As a familiar slogan says, "God doesn't make any junk." God is here for us to talk things out, he's here to listen. You are your best tool for self-help when you sit down with paper and pen, making two columns or pages. The heading for one could be "WHAT I WANT MOST IN MY LIFE" and the other "WHAT I CANNOT ACCEPT OR TOLERATE." Number about ten lines. Arrange your answers. One should be the "most important" or the "most non-negotiable." Women with children usually respond, "My children." To others, it may be marriage, a job, or a boyfriend. We live in a materialistic world. If we lack strong spiritual values, our concerns may be about money. It is useful to note that the life we live is in itself a ministry. Making money a chief concern has proven to be a fatal mistake. Numerous corporate executives can attest to the truth in this statement. It isn't only corporate ladder climbers who get misled in money's quest. Anyone can become trapped. They let their jobs take precedence over everything else. A single mom may get so involved in providing for her kids that she forgets who the real provider is. Her children need more than just more physical comforts or the latest "in" clothes or toys. In the picture, a woman should place greater emphasis on where her child is. She should focus on the spiritual, moral, and emotional development of her offspring. Agencies are in place to help women. They can have children or not. The agencies help them leave abuse and bad situations. We must remember that we are not alone in our fight. Others have experienced pain and are willing to be there to help us. Knowing that God, who cares deeply, is waiting for us to talk to Him, changes everything we might say.

Getting out of the bad situation is only the first step. Once in a safe place, we can look in retrospect and assess our decisions. Assessment should aid in not repeating the same bad choices. It is the choices we make that set into motion everything that happens to us. Returning to our prototype, ask: "When first moving out on your own, did you have a roommate? Who was she? When and where did you meet? What kind of person was she? Promiscuous? Or moral? What friends did she have? Returning to the boyfriend, did he begin to press you for sex right away? Or was it you? Did he drink alcoholic beverages, smoke cigarettes or pot, or do drugs?" You get the idea. Be objective. No one is asking you to judge him or her. How well did you know them? If you don't know the answer to a question, write down "don't know." After you have resettled, having moved to safety, you can go back and reprioritize. You can answer the questions that before were vague.

Okay. So, that woman doesn't even remotely resemble you or your circumstances. Let's review another scenario. You have been in and out of relationships, regardless of your marital status or money. Married and divorced one, two, three times? Or in and out again with significant others? Each one began with great enthusiasm but rapidly deteriorated. What caused it to fail? You tried to do everything right, be a faithful wife or partner, good homemaker. Why did it go wrong? Hmmmm. How long had you known each other? Really know each other? Where did you meet? Were you intimate before marriage? "Of course! Isn't everybody?" is a common response. Where do you go together? Bars? Church? Work? Grocery? What kind of friends do you and he have/cultivate? Was he single, separated, married, or divorced? What attracted you? Love? Lust? Loneliness? Friendship? Do you share a vision for life together? Are you in love with each other, or the idea of being with someone? Or, are you in lust? I reiterate. Marriage is a ministry. It is a sacred covenant. It is meant to be a blood covenant in the full biblical sense. God's word is filled with instruction on both a man's and a woman's role in a marriage. It is one that goes beyond procreation and carnal gratification. Marriage is an equal partnership. Each person complements the other's strengths and weaknesses. It is in the joining of the two parts of a whole that makes a complete unit.

If the relationship fails to meet both people's needs, each person needs to examine themselves. Your and your spouse's emotional, spiritual, and physical health reflect your life. Your health will also reflect the sort of mate you have or are. The health of your mate or your children can reflect how well you are fulfilling your part in their lives.

Make a new list of your priorities. Review and compare them to the original list. Apply the same questions used in the earlier scenario. Be honest with yourself. Should your mate wish to work with you, examining himself, GREAT! But your notes are for you alone. You may compare priority lists to see if you share the same vision for life. But, don't count on it. He may even think there is no problem, or if he does, may disagree with what you think it is. Rarely do men and women have the same interpretation or definition for a word or situation. Do you COMMUNICATE? Do you have the same understanding of what relationship, commitment, and romance mean? Keep in mind communication is a two-way dialogue. Each person speaks AND each person listens to the other. Are you both listening? As in the earlier example go to Failure #1, write down your responses. Move on to relationships #2 and #3, etc. until you have reached your current circumstances. Place the pages side by side. Compare one to the other in retrospect. Do you see a pattern developing?

Still not seeing anything resembling your circumstances? This third example is one that happens all too frequently in modern society. It involves violence and generations of violence and abuse. The abuse could be physical, mental, or sexual in nature. Any of these are senseless crimes of violence. A household may experience more than one at any given time. For the sake of clarification, they will be viewed separately.

You have been a victim of rape or molestation. These are never justifiable. As a result, you may feel dirty, violated, robbed, or confused. The attack or attacks may or may not have been documented. The assault may have been because of your choice of friends. Or, it may have been a random act of selection. It had nothing to do with you. The attacker, in over half of such cases, is a member of, or close friend of, the victim's family. The point to be made is; the attacker has stolen a private and precious part of your being. You could feel scared, ashamed, or alone. Whether you were a virgin or not is irrelevant. You have suffered an injury in body, mind, and spirit that is without logic. You go through feelings that lower your esteem. They say that no decent person will ever want anything to do with you if they learn of your defilement. You have lost self-esteem and you live a life of fear that someone may learn your 'dirty' secret. You have become a prisoner of your fears. In your attempt to hide the past, it controls you. You feel that you have to put on a façade. No one may see through it, even if it's not the real you. Are you making the right decision? Or, are you hiding behind a mask?

You have lived for so long in a house where you were told you will never amount to anything. You were also told the only thing you are any good for is to wait on someone else for his or her sexual pleasures. You accepted it as your fate in life. In your mind, you have been told you can never rise above the poverty or shame of a bad environment. And, you believe it and therefore never try. This is mental abuse. It is also mental abuse if you are told you'll always be fat or skinny. Or that you'll be an alcoholic or drug user. Or a prostitute or someone who freely sleeps around. That you believe and accept it is your choice.

You are physically abused when being sexually abused. But, physical abuse can also be sleep or food or healthcare deprivation. It can be being struck or pushed or denied adequate shelter. It can also be made to use drugs or alcohol. Or, it can be exposed to them by forced contact. For example, by breathing marijuana smoke, other drugs, or fumes from aerosols.

All the above can come in many forms. That you are exposed to or endure them may not have been in your control. But, to continue in them IS your choice.

A farmer knows that if he plants corn, he can't expect to harvest beans. Similarly, in life, we reap what we sow. It's crucial to recognize that we cannot expect different outcomes from the same actions. To navigate our challenges, we can acknowledge that what we are doing might be wrong. But then, what is the right approach? A hard pill to swallow is that we can't learn what to do from things that don't work. So, what worked for me? I turned to the Bible for guidance and wisdom. A learned man, a Pharisee, and later a disciple of Christ wrote: "…whatsoever a man (or woman) sows, that he shall also reap." (See Galatians 6:7.) Where we seek our companions usually designates the interests. Are you a woman or man seeking a faithful, loving mate? Why would you pick up someone in a bar, a prostitute, or a casino? In Proverbs, King Solomon's ageless wisdom bears witness to the principles and problems of daily life. They are the same ones that we face today. The world is no different today than it was in Solomon's time. In 400 B.C., the big problems were prostitution, drunkenness, and disrespectful youth. Also, there were theft, murder, idolatry, and witchcraft. The people who left Egypt in 1450 B.C. faced the same problems. They surrounded Lot at Sodom in 1898 B.C. They challenged the people of Corinth in 59 A.D. The only differences were the places, clothes, and transport.

One day at a time, or one small step at a time is better than attempting to solve all your difficulties at once. Too much can be overwhelming and lead to depression. You may find yourself feeling as if your mind is numb. But, that is better than crying, and your head aching and feeling filled with sand. Depression leaves you exhausted and usually gives you a headache. Do you want to know how old your predicament is? In circa 2 or 3 A.D., Jesus told a woman of Samaria about her promiscuous life. She had lived with numerous men. The man she was with was not her spouse. To remedy her problem, the solution was simply to 'sin no more.' In our terms, stop doing what you're doing. This text will say a lot, 'the choice is yours.' You can make the changes and live a happy life.

Today, you are starting a new adventure. It will change how you think and what you accept. You are going to find your true potential and stop running in fear, hiding in your shame. You will learn about yourself and reshaping your life. This will usher in a time for finding your potential and your hidden gifts. You'll also learn how to realize your dreams. The materials you are covering are known to benefit all who have applied them. Each person is uniquely different. You are uniquely different. No one is exactly like you. You were born for this time to live a happy life. It's a life of fulfillment, no matter your current situation or status. You will no doubt have heard the saying that God 'owns the cattle of a thousand hills.' It is biblical in origin, but I would like to add that he owns the dirt they stand on and the grass they eat as well. He sees quite well to their needs and will adroitly handle your every need also. Stop beating yourself up. Haven't you had enough of that kind of life?

The existence you know now is a lie. It is not who you are or what you can be. There is a doorway to lead you into a better space. In that space, there is no shame and denial. You can control your emotions, even depression. Look, this isn't to say you aren't going to have to work at it or that you will have a life free from troubles. What it is saying is that you can take back your life. It is everyone's desire to succeed in life. How can anyone succeed when they are unhappy, even miserable? How can you find contentment or love with anyone, when you are still a prisoner to some event or thing from the past? Do not be afraid to step into the light. Like a blind man who first regains sight, in the beginning, the light can be painful and you may not see clearly at first. Yet, when the sight adjusts to the light, what excitement and rejoicing!

It's time to stop believing the destructive lies. Forget all the meaningless drivel that has been spewed at you. You are a beautiful and desirable person. You have no reason to feel inferior to other people. There are no big 'I's' and little 'U's'. We are all equal. If you are short or fat or tall or thin and are mocked for it, you can rebut by saying: "Shorter people are just more lovable. You're just jealous." You fill in the blank. Get your head up out of the proverbial sand. You certainly are not alone. Everyone has flaws.

You are tired of life as it is, or you would not be searching these pages. You ache for more than you are experiencing. You want to live free: free of the shackles caused by the lifestyle you lead and the chains of your past. The dank dungeon of your prison has all but blocked out every faint beam of light to your soul. Your lungs ache for fresh air. The air is not heavy with mold and mildew. It comes from the decaying world you live in. The filthy rags of your incarceration are threadbare and tattered. You long to bathe in freshness, as cool and clean as a mountain stream in springtime. You are the captivating butterfly about to burst forth from its unsightly cocoon.

You try to hide your feelings of shame and

degradation by putting on a mask, a false façade. You try to pretend that it doesn't exist, as if nothing had occurred. But, it keeps coming back to you, like an offensive odor in your face. You recognize it in the way you respond or interact with men, and in your personal appearance. It is there you carry your wounds. Their words cause painful, seared scars you hide within. You are always afraid to trust, to share yourself. You are a prisoner within your own mind. It is apparent to you that every man you encounter only wants to take more from you. It is easier to give in than to explain why you are hesitant to become close to anyone. Cheap sex, not love, that's safer. Or, is it a big smokescreen? You aren't looking for commitment. You use their old lines. Just looking for a good time, don't call me. I'll call you. You're a liberated, modern woman. Yeah, right. So when is it liberating or modern to inflict more grief on you than has already been dumped on you? You have deceived yourself. You believe you have nothing left to give but the sex they all want, no strings attached. It's all men ever want or think about, isn't it? You can't feel any dirtier than you do now. Or can you? The only difference between you and a whore is that she gets paid.

Stop Right There! You are somebody! You have worth. Oh, you may never know by whom or why you were attacked. But, you have value, no matter how many men have misused you and moved on to another woman. You aren't alone. Bad things happen to good people.

You survived. It is time to move on, defeat the evil that was done to you. You can't crawl into the proverbial hole and pull it in after you. You were a child or an adult. You did not ask the person(s) to violate and misuse you (and it's certain that you did not). What happened is not your fault. There is a beautiful and valuable person inside you. She is dying to come into the sunlight. She's living in shadow that is slowly and surely destroying her.

All those so-called friends meant well. They told you, "you must have asked for it" or "you just weren't clear enough saying no" or "you should have screamed." But, they were mouthing mindless platitudes. They had never been in that situation. And they are not your friends. It is probable that even family members may not, despite what they say, hold your best interests. What you do need are friends who will help build you up; help you move beyond your past. You are more than one event. Yet, many women carry their pain of the attack a lifetime, unable to talk about the cause of their soul-deep grief. They may have attempted to talk early on, but were told things like "Just forget it." Or "You're just making that up." This has closed open lines of discussion. Try to understand this. Family and friends fear a reality they can't understand or accept. They are in denial.

Denial is a term frequently discussed in psychological circles. More than just a word, denial represents a state of mind where an individual fails to accept the reality of their situation. This mindset often leads to a refusal to accept that their actions are connected to others reactions. Those in denial blame others for their problems. They never look inward. So they miss the opportunity to understand how they could change their circumstances.

To move past victimhood and towards healing, it is crucial to admit that no one is perfect and that mistakes are a natural part of life. Holding onto the anger and pain inflicted by others keeps a person trapped in their own mental prison. Instead, recognize that while you cannot change the past, you can control how you respond to it moving forward. Accepting and learning from past mistakes is a vital step in personal growth.

Children learn behaviors by observing the adults around them. Before understanding words, they watch our actions. If they see a parent constantly acting like a victim, they are likely to imitate this behavior. It's crucial to recognize that violence, denial, and negativity are learned behaviors, which means they can also be unlearned. This change doesn't come from simply telling a child, 'Do as I say, not as I do,' but from changing your own actions as well. How you talk and react to things matters. By choosing to move beyond past traumas, we can start healing and break the cycle of victimhood. Encourage resilience and positive behavior by modeling strength and recovery for your children.

Even those who have endured horrific acts like molestation or rape can find a way to move forward. It's important to understand that these events, as terrible as they are, do not define you. Acknowledge the pain, but also recognize your strength and resilience. Forgiving the perpetrator, while difficult, can be a powerful step towards freeing yourself from the past. This doesn't mean forgetting or condoning their actions, but rather releasing the hold they have on your life.

True healing often requires support from those who understand your pain. Seek out individuals or support groups who have faced similar struggles and have found a way to overcome them. Remember, you are no longer a victim; you are a survivor with the power to reclaim your life.

You are alive. When I realized that God made it possible for me to be in this world, I understood I wasn't created by accident. It's incredible to think how many times it could have been my last day. By any reasonable or logical thinking, it feels good to believe that God wanted you here. To believe we are still alive for a reason. **GOD WANTED YOU! YOU! YOU! YOU!** If He made you, then He still wants you. Otherwise, you wouldn't have survived the ordeals you have endured. You wouldn't be here, just as I once thought I wouldn't be. Now, you have a rare chance. You can be there for others who don't feel loved. You can understand their pain because you survived it. You are a beacon of hope for others because you understand. So, there must be a greater plan for your life than just existing. Recognize that you have worth because you've survived what others haven't.

As you work through your pain, be kind and honest with yourself. Write down your thoughts and feelings, making lists of your priorities and goals. This process can help clarify what you truly want out of life and what changes you need to make to achieve it. Keep your lists updated as you grow and evolve, and don't be afraid to seek out new sources of support and guidance.

You are worthy of love, respect, and happiness. Believe in yourself and your ability to create a life that reflects your true worth.

The Faces of Depression

Depression wears many masks, often manifesting as a profound sense of worthlessness and isolation. I would wake up each day with thoughts like, "Why me? Why can't anyone see what I'm going through? Why does everyone seem to focus on what's wrong in my life rather than what I've done right?" If this sounds familiar, I want you to know you're not alone. These feelings isolate us, making us feel as though we're trapped.

Self-Worth and Isolation

For many, depression erodes self-worth, leading to thoughts like, "My life is as useless as spoiled milk. I'm worthless, confused, and everything I touch seems to go wrong. Everyone around me seems to want a piece of me. Why was I born? I'd be better off dead." I know how these thoughts can trap you in a cycle of self-deprecation and hopelessness.

Depression convinces you that you are less than others, fostering deep-seated insecurities. Questions like, "Why is everyone around me angry all the time? I'm not beautiful. Why does everyone act as though they are better than me?" reflect this internal struggle, making you feel isolated and inferior.

38

Biblical Perspectives

These feelings of despair aren't new. Solomon wisely said, "There is nothing new under the sun." Passages like Job 10 and Psalm 39 in the Bible reflect on human suffering and the search for meaning. They remind us that others have faced similar struggles and found ways to cope.

To overcome depression, you must confront the person in the mirror. Acknowledge your misery and understand that these feelings are not permanent. As John 8:32 states, "And you shall know the truth, and the truth shall make you free." Facing the truth about your depression is the first step toward liberation.

Impact on Relationships

Depression impacts relationships deeply. Thoughts like, "Is there no end to my problems? When will I get a break? No one appreciates me," are common. Depression's cycle can make you feel trapped, as if you're always spinning your wheels and going nowhere.

You want to be a good parent, a loving spouse, a dedicated employee. You don't need wealth; you just want a happy, fulfilling life. Yet, depression convinces you that this is unattainable. King David offers hope in Psalm 30:5, "Weeping may last for a night, but joy comes in the morning." This reminds us that suffering is temporary and that joy is possible.

Societal Influences

Today's society often belittles the home and craves brutal pleasures, much like the decline of the Roman Empire. Poor choices in friends, jobs, diet, recreation, and relationships all contribute to our struggles. Recognizing this broader context can help in understanding our personal battles.

Illness can trigger depression, leading to a focus on immediate suffering rather than future prospects. Thoughts like, "No one cares about me unless it benefits them. Why does it matter if I bathe or change clothes?" can lead to severe neglect of self-care and a desire to give up.

Understanding the Depths

If you relate to these feelings, you understand the pain behind them. For those who don't, imagine the tiredness of a long illness combined with complete isolation and hopelessness. This is the reality for many who suffer from depression.

Hope and Faith

Suicide is a top cause of death among those suffering from depression, often seen as the only escape. Yet, there is hope in the saving grace of faith. People who have found solace in prayer and faith share their experiences, showing that there is a way out, even from the darkest depths.

"Why am I here? Why was I ever born?" Ecclesiastes 3:1-2 addresses these big questions, reminding us that each thing has its time. Perhaps the question should be, "What is my purpose?" Understanding that there is a divine plan can offer comfort and direction.

Finding True Happiness

What is happiness, and how can one find it? Ecclesiastes shows Solomon's wisdom. It says true joy comes from seeking peace and kindness, and avoiding vainglory. Temporary pleasures often lead to emptiness. Lasting joy comes from meaningful pursuits.

Depression is a multifaceted condition, often triggered by a combination of factors. While faith and self-reflection are important, seeking professional help is crucial. Therapy, medication, and support groups can help fight depression. They provide the tools needed to do so.

Remember, you are not alone in this struggle. Many have faced similar battles and emerged stronger. With spiritual guidance and professional help, you can heal and find joy in life.

In the next sections, we will cover practical steps and spiritual guidance. They will help you navigate depression and find the joy and purpose you seek.

PART 2

Whew! Now we're getting somewhere! If you've skipped over Part I to dive right in, I urge you to go back. There are no shortcuts. The foundation you build in Part I is essential. Now, we're stepping into an unknown, unfamiliar zone. Taking action is a step of faith. What is faith? It is the "assured expectation of things hoped for."

You've made your lists of priorities and unacceptable situations. You've determined why you are hurting and what you want out of life. Are you ready to do something about it? Change requires commitment, and it won't happen all at once. Skip a few pages in your notebook and write "My Gifts/Talents" at the top. Draw in a deep, slow breath, and exhale slowly. Can't think of any? Close your eyes, lean back, and relax for a minute. We all have gifts. It's as simple as thinking about what you do best.

Here are a few examples to get you thinking about what you do best; the things that make you feel happy and fulfilled:

My Gifts/Talents

Make friends easily   —————————————

Caring   —————————————

Helpful/compassionate   —————————————

Good listener   —————————————

Charitable   —————————————

Motivator/leader   —————————————

Dependable   —————————————

Punctual   —————————————

Musical   —————————————

Artistic   —————————————

Sew   —————————————

Cook   —————————————

Neat/orderly   —————————————

Problem solver   —————————————

Industrious   —————————————

Friendly and outgoing

No gift is too great or too small to put on the list. Rank your gifts from best to worst based on your perspective, not on what others may think. Whether you're good with children or older people, that is a gift. Some people consider it a small thing to be friendly and put another at ease, but to a stranger in a new area, a warm greeting is a real blessing. Not everyone can talk to a total stranger and be warm, sincere, and welcoming.

Some people have a gift for caring. They care for those confined in hospitals, nursing homes, or who are home-bound. They visit strangers to give them a ray of sunshine. There may be Christian Youth Centers or other community programs where you live, often crying out for volunteers. Young people from single-parent homes or homes where both parents work need these programs to create their own activities. In community centers, the young and old can socialize and play games, learning good moral values with guidance. Most centers are free to the youth and are operated by volunteers and supported by donations.

Narrow it down even more. Has someone moved into your neighborhood? Are you the kind of person who introduces yourself and offers to help them find their way around? Or, seeing little ones, do you take over a few cookies and say, "Welcome to the neighborhood. Maybe these will keep the little guys busy while you're unpacking."

If you're a craftsperson, do you make small gifts for children, the elderly, or the homeless? Your leadership skills may let you organize a Community Food Bank.

You could also run an After-School Program for kids whose parents work late.

Age is not a factor. For example, a seventy-two-year-old woman from Concord, North Carolina, volunteers for 'Meals on Wheels.' She says, "I take food to old people." A good cook might make a dozen cookies and take them to a homeless shelter. When asked why you'd do such a thing, your response might be like the woman from Concord: "because Jesus loves me and He loves you, too." You don't need to preach a sermon to let someone know that somebody cares about them.

A retired couple from Florida visits inmates for hours. They bring a message: it's never too late to ask for forgiveness. They aren't paid, nor are they evangelists or ordained ministers. When people call them kooks, they merely reply, "Yes, I know."

None of the foregoing examples were missionaries or preachers. They are ordinary people who overcame obstacles and found a way to add joy into the world. One of the hardest things you'll probably ever do is forgive the people who hurt you. It may appear to be impossible right now, but it does happen. It is part of the healing process. At this time, you may feel like giving up. The process could even seem to be going nowhere or be too difficult. Don't quit! All the writing keeps you focused on your goals – YOUR goals, no one else's. It will be worth all the work. Teachers say writing keeps you focused. It also helps memory by using many senses.

First, you must see where you made the wrong choices. Then, commit to doing whatever it takes to change your life. The next step is to see your strengths (gifts). This will give you more confidence to handle harder changes. As a teen, you had an entire spectrum of aspirations. One, no doubt, appealed more than the others. What was it? Do you still feel strongly about it? There was a plan for your life from the day you were conceived.

Authority

It is wise to remind yourself not to fall into denial of the existence of a problem. If we don't make a habit of slowing down and reflecting on truly good advice, we can find ourselves in the weeds. We can figure things out by reflecting on all the good advice we have absorbed over our lifetime.

One might say, "I have a serious problem; what is one way I could overcome it?" or "God will help me overcome this." Without religious texts, we are left trying to figure everything out on our own. Making a habit of talking with God helps us keep our relationship with Him strong during hard times.

Seeking Guidance and Reflection

A good therapist helps you to no longer need them. Similarly, having a regular practice of reflection or prayer, moving in a positive direction becomes natural. Without developing a relationship with yourself or a higher power, there's a tendency to easily slip back into old ways. Habits created through faith or principles, endure during the tough times. They are something we can rely on when everything else is failing. Additionally, we become aware of others who are also striving to make the best decisions. Community builds support.

Community and Personal Growth

Granted, communities, including churches, can sometimes be filled with hypocritical people. But isn't that the reason they gather? To become better people in the first place? Seeing people as they are isn't the problem; it's each of us being unaware of our own flaws. The goal is to change our behavior, not just repeat good advice. True learning means changing what we do and how we react.

Outward Seeking Help

The misconception is that one can demand a higher power. Or, one can rely on others without taking action. While support systems and higher powers can aid us, they are not there to fulfill demands without our effort. Requests for help should be made with humility, not entitlement. From an external perspective, this approach leads to discovering answers. When you figure out what you need to do, it isn't by accident but by design. By being willing to make changes, you gain the insights to create those changes yourself. Whether you are speaking to God or reflecting on your own, humility is essential in addressing your problems. Discuss your problems, and answers will emerge.

The If-Then Relationship with Support

The heavenly Father is an 'if-then' God. When you draw near to Him, He will bless you. Being 'grounded in God's word' is a requisite to receiving all He has for blessing you. It's more than just turning on a religious TV program once in a while or sitting in a church pew. It requires a serious commitment to praying, studying, confessing, repenting, and changing. Personal effort must be made. Learning is not achieved through osmosis.

Returning to the Source

Having clarified these points, come back to the source of authority. The Bible? A particular denomination? Doctrine? The authority rests in none other than the author and finisher of our faith: Jesus Christ. The church is our Mother on earth. It nurtures and feeds us. Jesus' teachings help us learn how to react. The closer we act as Jesus did, the more we will be remembered. It is that simple. It is a juncture where it is possible to gain insight and become familiar with God's guide for living. One church could leave you flat. Another invigorates and leaves you feeling better about being alive. As your insight grows, you will find yourself automatically making changes to your life. A church will shape your destiny if you add it into your life. You may even make new friends. Do not be alarmed to find yourself led to change where you go to church. Physical changes occur when you grow into what YOU want.

Choosing the Right Support System

There are many non-orthodoxies and pseudo-Christian denominations. Most of these groups do not encourage individual study. They publish their own Bible translations and forbid the use of or comparison to other translations. Some declare the Bible to be a book of myths. To illuminate on the variations further would deviate from our course. See the reference section at the end of this book for information on these.

At first, it would be easier to affiliate with a known denomination. Some traditional denominations are listed alphabetically: Assemblies of God, Baptist, Catholic, Church of God, Episcopal, Methodist, and Presbyterian. When you make a choice, know that the goal is to be better for yourself and your community. Getting caught up in a church that has turned its visitors into profit is something to be aware of.

Congratulations! You have come a long way if you have applied each step in getting to this section. Before we start the next phase of our trip, consider a hypothetical but typical situation. Our model is based on real people and situations. She may resemble someone you know, but she is a hypothetical composite. Her life, like your own, will have clear differences. But, each case should not be so far off as to prevent practical application. All events here are real, but they come from two or more actual events or cases that were similar. Kelly Jones is fictitious.

"Long ago, there lived a girl, in a land far away."

Kelly Jones, 5'5", 145 lbs., was born between 1950 and 1975. Her exact age is irrelevant. She was born to middle-class, baby-boomer parents, who shared the post-war lust for life. Kelly, herself, is a confused by-product of the sexual revolution. Her race or ethnicity can be whatever you want it to be. Memories of her dysfunctional family are few. Those memories she had were mostly of being shut up in her room, so her parents could 'talk.' Talking was generally one-sided, in our case, by her mom. She could rarely make out the words, but they were angry and shrill as her mother's voice rose. The anger was unmistakable. Kelly could never clearly hear enough words, so she concluded it was something she had done. She was closed in her room, the way she was when she was being punished, and mommy was mad. As time passed, when Kelly was alone with her mommy, she began 'walking on eggshells.' It never occurred to Kelly that it was daddy that mommy was angry with. Kelly didn't like it when her mother got mad because it always meant that her daddy would go away. In her mind, if she didn't make mommy mad, there would be no more yelling and daddy wouldn't leave again. She missed daddy. Kelly could recall one time when her daddy had come home every night for a while. But, then came the day when her mother got really mad. She had to sit on a chair and face the corner until her daddy came home. She pondered the wall. She couldn't understand what had made her mommy so angry. She didn't know why her mommy had screamed at her and hit her over and over, then put her in the corner. Daddy did come home. He was late. He'd been in an accident, but he was all right. Kelly was sent to her room. Soon, daddy went away again. Although his departure had nothing to do with her alleged behavior, Kelly did not know it. Kelly was taken to Granny Nellie's house. Mommy left. Kelly was small and didn't know what she had done to make no one want her. She recalled some of the words mommy used: evil, wicked, and unappreciative. She couldn't pronounce them well and had absolutely no idea what they meant. Whatever it was, it must be really bad. She had heard mommy scream them, sometimes from the other room and sometimes at Kelly. Another thing she could not yet grasp was marital problems. She tried to remember the angry words. If she could learn what they meant, then maybe she could change. Mommy would be happy. Then she and daddy could come home again.

TIME-OUT

Let's review some of the problems taking shape in Kelly's profile.

Children should never be exposed to loud arguments between parents. Maintaining a child's safe space through private, calm discussions and disagreements is crucial. When a child overhears an argument, it's important for both parents to apologize. Because children often don't understand the context of the argument, they usually blame themselves. Therefore, parents should reassure the child that everything is under control.

If a disagreement is overheard, sit down with the child and explain, "We're sorry you heard that. Sometimes adults disagree, but it's not your fault, and we love you very much." This can make a big difference. Kelly's parents didn't explain their fights or reassure her, leaving her confused and feeling unworthy.

Kelly's parents either thought she was too young to care about their problems or didn't consider her feelings at all. It's important to always acknowledge that children, even at a young age, can sense tension and conflict. Explaining the situation helps them understand better and feel secure.

Sending Kelly to her room made her feel like she was being punished and that the arguments were because of her. Instead, reassure children during conflicts that the disagreement is between the adults and not about the child's behavior. The best thing a child can experience is witnessing an argument being resolved.

A lack of touch and acceptance can make children feel unloved and delay their emotional growth. Regular hugs, kisses, and kind words show children they are loved and valued. Children often drift through life seeking the nurturing they missed in childhood. Regularly affirming your love and acceptance helps foster their self-esteem and emotional security.

Parents can get caught up in their own issues, forgetting that children are also affected. Being mindful of your actions and words around children is crucial. Remember, they are observing and learning from you, mimicking behaviors rather than following instructions. Children try to figure out what they are allowed to do long before they learn what words mean.

Maintaining calm discussions around children is crucial. Explaining that conflicts are not their fault makes them feel loved, secure, and valued. This approach promotes healthy emotional development and mitigates the negative impacts of parental conflict. Parents can practice handling conflicts in low-stress situations for greater success. When stressed and confused, we all tend to *avoid* rather than **overcome** challenges.

CO-DEPENDENCY

Without ever learning how to resolve conflicts or have calm discussions, our relationships suffer. Codependency is the condition relationships fall into when participants never solve problems or improve together. These relationships are generally shallow and sex-based. A victim is always crushed by the failure of each relationship and never seems to see why they failed. They have low self-esteem. They hope, each time, it will be different. Feeling ugly, unworthy, and inadequate, they become jaded with life. They conclude that the unstable world in which they exist is all there is to living. They do not see the need to seek help. A problem exists, but they don't recognize it. This is a vicious cycle that repeats across generations.

The greatest victims are the children who grow up knowing no other lifestyle. Lack of touch and acceptance causes a child to be emotionally delayed. The parent will see the child as unable to take responsibility, act, or make good decisions. This further nurtures the problem by hindering the child's mental growth.

Visits to Kelly's mother were rare. Meetings with her father were rarer. Hesitant at first, Kelly grew close to her grandmother, her sanctuary. Just as she would settle into a routine, her mother would disrupt it with promises of reuniting their family. These fleeting reunions, lasting a week or a month, always ended the same. Kelly would be alone in her room, the walls echoing with loud arguments as her father left once more. Each time, her mother would say, "Your father doesn't want us." Over time, Kelly began to believe her mother didn't want her either. Once again, she was left at Granny Nellie's house. Granny Nellie was Kelly's anchor, her presence a steadying force in a chaotic world. It was Granny who taught Kelly to love herself, her parents, and about God. Her grandmother always valued education, even though she never got the opportunity to study beyond third grade. Kelly faced firsthand the bigotry and prejudice toward a multi-racial child. At Granny's, she found the love she craved, and her self-esteem was strengthened. In Nellie's house, she found the courage to face prejudice. It was Granny who encouraged her to set goals. She believed she could achieve anything if she worked hard. Kelly was determined to be the best. She quickly grasped her studies. Soon, she was first in her class academically. She made the Principal's List and the National Honor Society.

On the surface, Kelly was a healthy, normal child. She was exceptional academically. The only clue to an underlying problem was seen in close observation. Kelly was a quiet and withdrawn child. Though she excelled academically, Kelly had no friends. Entering puberty, Kelly had no interest in dating or socializing like her peers. She went along with group activities when urged. Her driving goal was the one she had set at age four, when she had been unceremoniously dropped at her grandmother Nellie's.

"...All the love in her heart she would give..."

She would make her parents want her. She would earn their respect and admiration. She would make them love her. She would make herself more lovable, so they would see she was not the awful words she grew to know the meaning of. The next turn of events was one that would rock Kelly's world. Granny became ill suddenly. The older woman was never sick; she was the one who always took care of others. Where was Kelly to go? Granny Nellie just as suddenly died. Kelly was fifteen! She had no one now. Amid the flurry of activity surrounding the funeral, nobody noticed the stoic-set, young face or the fact that Kelly never cried. She somehow got moved into her mother's residence. It was all a blur to her. Kelly focused on school, throwing herself at her studies. In a few months, Kelly would be sixteen. She found a job and began paying the required room and board to her mother. Her room was an enclosed back porch. It was small but adequate. It held a twin-size bed, a small bureau, and a gas space heater. Kelly remained withdrawn. Her daddy had visited twice for a few minutes. Neither father nor daughter had time to become acquainted. They were total strangers. Nor did her mother take the time to know the strange girl.

People with a romantic nature would anticipate a fairy tale, slow recovery, and the reconciling of a family. But life isn't always forgiving. Like many dysfunctional homes, nothing had changed. The only difference was the age of the participants and the addition of a couple of siblings. Kelly hardly knew them. She had hoped to earn the respect, if not the love, of her mother. It never happened. In the daily routine of the home, Kelly was always the "odd one." Maybe her mother couldn't show affection. Or, she felt awkward with the child she'd abandoned. Kelly just never fit in. She could cook, clean, work, and go to school. Yet, no matter what she did, or how well, it was met with, "...all right, but it would be quicker, differently, better if so-and-so had helped..." It was no surprise when Kelly graduated in the top ten in her class of four hundred. She was the first in her family to complete high school. Then, she was at the top of her class at business school. But no one noticed.

Kelly had been the first in her family, since they had immigrated to America in the 1600s, to attend college. Her 3.9-grade average caught no one in her family's attention. Kelly became the achiever. Her pursuits consumed her attention. Ridiculed for her extremely limited dating, she began going to nightclubs, drinking hard liquors. Was she only twenty? Bartenders never asked her about her age. She felt numb and emotionless. It made her look older, haunted. Love? Dreams? Those concepts were distant, nebulous things. She never dared dwell on such frivolous ideas or even hope of meeting the proverbial Prince Charming. She would cynically add, '**who would want to spend a lifetime with her?**' Nor could Kelly envision such a relationship. She had heard tales about her granny's happy marriage. That sort of thing was the stuff of fairytales; it didn't happen in this day and time. She had no time for fairytales. Any closeness seemed dangerous, threatening.

Her contemporaries were getting married, starting families. They chattered about love, wedding plans, and suchlike. It was all babble and meant nothing to Kelly. Her world had become school, work, and worship. Worship was peculiar. It was not the stuff of traditional Christianity, like the places she'd gone with her grandmother.

Kelly merely tagged along with her mother and siblings. She had hoped if she went along she would somehow fit in.

When Granny had been alive, she was a part of something. Her mother's church bore no resemblance to the one where she had attended with her grandmother. Once more, she was a square peg among round ones. She asked too many questions in the Bible study group, and the answers she received did not add up to what she read in the same text. Some had even alluded to her difference as '**not from around here.**'

Her mother and siblings began to press her to '**settle down and raise a family.**' They were always throwing her at someone. Eighteen or thirty-eight, any man was fair game. His only requirement was to be single. They just wanted her to get married. A young man at her mother's church began compelling her to marry him after only a two-week acquaintance. Kelly felt like she was trapped in a vice, the pressure from all sides squeezing the life out of her. After a month, she acquiesced. But she had doubts. On a trip to meet his family, he raped her. Confused and scared, not knowing what to do, she went home. Home? There was no one she could talk to. And no one noticed or asked about her feelings. They were excited, planning her wedding. They would be rid of her. In all fairness, they believed it was all in Kelly's best interest. Her reluctance, when she tried to express it, was brushed aside as '**cold feet.**' She was simply pushed along by the avalanche of everyone else's plans. Her fiancé wanted to move up the date. Striving to be optimistic, Kelly rationalized the attack as uncontrolled passion. What else could it be? She didn't know anything about sex, and his assault was her first experience with it. Her pale, drawn face and dampened spirit were labeled '**wedding day jitters.**' Kelly was determined to put the attack behind her and move ahead. There was no one she felt she could discuss it with, and it could not be changed. What she didn't know was that this was only the beginning of her troubles.

She missed her grandmother. How many times had she longed to talk with her about everything? She wished the old woman whom she adored could be here to guide her in this major move. To think of her beloved mentor still caused a sharp pain in her heart. Had she really been gone five years? The sadness was deep, and she still hadn't wept. Kelly never cried, facing every trauma stoically. Her resolve never crumbled. She could not have said, even as she was walked down the aisle by a father she hardly knew, that she was in love with the man she was about to marry. She would have gladly run the other way but felt trapped. She wanted to be loved just like everyone else. But that only meant she was in love with the idea of being loved. When abuse began in her own marriage, she hid a lot of her pain. Wasn't it normal when people were angry? Was that why she had been kept in her room when her parents argued? Kelly felt empty inside and alone. There was a gaping void, and neither marriage nor any other human relationship could fill it. The pain and emptiness were too deep.

TIME-OUT

Reviewing the latest events, it is poignantly clear that the pattern was set in childhood and is being repeated in adulthood. But, the pattern didn't begin in Kelly's childhood; it is much older. Kelly's father spent his first thirteen years in a dysfunctional home. His father walked out when difficulties arose. Kelly's mother's childhood was hard, though not from friction in the home. Her anguish stemmed from the death of her father when she was three years old. There was no welfare system to fall back on, just a nation recovering from the Great Depression.

> "...But love wasn't in the hearts
> of people where she lived..."

The abuses in Kelly's marriage began verbally and escalated to physical within a few short months. It was the rejection she had endured from her parents as a child, in a different package. Her father had never struck her mother; it was her mother who struck out in anger physically.

First, she was raped. Then, a man she barely knew verbally and physically abused her. To him, she was little more than a slave. The abuse worsened when she became pregnant. Her controlling mate forbade her any contact with her family or to work. Her place was in the home, to care for his needs. Beatings grew worse and more frequent. Provocation could be a cold supper (due to his being late) or unfinished laundry. Most laundry was done by hand in the bathtub. Occasionally, he would allow her to go to the Laundromat, but she had to walk to and from it, carrying her loads of clothes. Morning sickness left her too weak to want the intimacy her mate demanded as '**his rights**'. Unhappy, Kelly tried to fight back and protect her baby. Publicly, he doted on her and never hit her. She knew she'd '**get it**' when she got home when he squeezed her in warning to be silent.

She made an attempt to get help from her mother's church. They brushed her aside with a vague remark about newlyweds needing to adjust. She tried to hide the bruises and made excuses when they could not be disguised: "I slipped and fell," or "I'm so clumsy." "I tripped over my own feet." She was a shadow of the girl she had been at fifteen. It was then that she, at least, had hopes and dreams, although hidden inside. Kelly is like thousands of women in the same predicament today, afraid to leave but living in misery. She spent her days trying to make everything perfect. That is, perfect by her husband's rules. Some of her '**duties**' were demeaning, even painful, degrading, and lascivious. Refusal to participate in sexual acts falling into these areas only brought a beating and forced compliance. Once more, Kelly felt worthless, unworthy of happiness. She began entertaining ideas of suicide, fantasizing about the release her death would bring. She fought hard to stop herself from these thoughts. "What would happen to my babies?" Fear is a jailer like no other.

The violence increased. She was afraid to sleep when her spouse was at home. She'd lie quietly, listening to

64

his breathing. Breakfast would be on the table before he got up. When he left for the day, Kelly cleaned up quickly and tended to her babies. Washing clothes by hand or stomping the dirt out in the bathtub, she hurried through her work. She needed sleep. She made a makeshift alarm to wake her, just in case he came home while she napped. She put the children down for their naps. She stacked pots and pans the eldest played with near the door. She put some noisy toys on top. They would fall loudly if the door opened. This was how she stole short, troubled sleep. She felt lucky that she never overslept and the alarm was never set off. He never learned about it.

Numerous broken bones and scars later, Kelly was nearing her breaking point. The final blow came when her spouse, whose perversion seemed to grow continually, wanted her to have sex with some of his friends so he could watch. She refused; for all it mattered to him. But he dropped it there, and Kelly thought she had finally won. Lulled into false security, she thought her refusal had been honored. He didn't hit her. He had changed the subject and began talking about wanting to work on their problems. Blindly, she allowed the children to go to his parents at his request, "so they could talk." Kelly was grasping at straws, a faint hope of something being changed. When he returned from dropping off the children, he indicated that he wanted her to "engage in a bit of fun." Alarms went off inside her head. That was what he had called his request for group sex. Her original refusal now met the violence previously absent. Knocked to the floor, she was kicked as she scrambled away. He would "make her learn to do what he told her." His assault continued until he had her nude and tied hands and feet to the bed. "There are ways to make you do whatever I want," he said. "You'll talk turkey if I tell you to before I'm done and do anything I say." A slap to her face accompanied the threat. He was enamored with the '**Executioner**' series paperback novels. He had made her listen to grotesque passages before and read them with relish. He was quoting even now. They were his personal handbooks for cruelty. He reveled in the torture extracted on its victims and in stories of the gulag German death camp means of persuasion. He took a cigarette lighter from his pocket and held the flame to her flesh, spot after spot, until each began to redden or blister. The flame threatened to ignite her pubic hair.

The old familiar stoicism was there; her armor. She refused to cry. He urinated while raping her. Her lack of any show of weakness infuriated him. Knocking broke his assault. He left her and put on loud music. What happened next, she tried blocking out mentally by staring blankly at the ceiling. Several men repeatedly raped her. She refused to respond as the twisted man she had married threatened her with knives and fire. The others laughed as though he was joking. If he killed her, she would not show fear, only contempt. The men laughed, drank, and smoked as their buddies tried to outdo each other in perversions as they raped and sodomized her. Kelly prayed silently. Day became night. When she passed out or fell asleep, being slapped brought her back to wakefulness. Another day, another night, another day. Kelly was sure she was dying. She felt a part of her (her soul?) leave her body and found herself hovering above the room and her body lying below. She watched as someone hit her; this time, she wasn't coming back. Swearing, one man felt for her pulse. She was quickly untied, and everyone left the house. She felt sorry for the girl below from where her soul hovered, but now a bright light beckoned. Kelly turned into the light, surrounded instantly by warm, soft colors and music that was at once inside and all around her, sweet and indefinable. She seemed to be rushing toward the light that grew brighter. She was aware that she was disembodied, and the intensity of the light never hurt her vision. She felt the weight of burdens falling away. Abruptly, the path to the light was barred. She must go back. She pleaded, "No." She tried seeing past the being that barred her path, the beauty of the figure emitting the light, and the colors refracting from what must be a wall. Her early faith told her that there stood the LORD. Instantly, she was back in her body, racked with pain. She fell several times getting to the bathroom. She ran water so hot it almost burned her flesh, scrubbing vigorously. But the feeling of filth would not leave. She dressed and drove to get her children. Her husband was '**fishing**,' she was told. Loading her children, Kelly returned to her house and threw a few clothes into the car. She guessed that her spouse was setting up an alibi and would come home to find her body. Boy, was he in for a surprise! She didn't know where to go. Hopefully, her mother would not turn her away. It was apparent she had been beaten. Escape had been narrow. Her mind felt numb. Thankfully, no questions were asked, or at least she had no recollection of any. She really had looked bad. She stayed long enough to get a job and pushed herself to the limits of physical endurance. Constantly afraid, never trusting anyone to give away her children's and her location. There were several days that she had been unconscious after arriving at her mother's house. A doctor had prescribed sedatives, although she couldn't remember going to see a doctor, that made her sleep at first. But fear was always before her. She moved frequently not to be found. Depression took control, affecting her judgment. She attempted suicide but failed. Everything she did, she failed, or so she thought. However, from somewhere deep inside her, there arose a spirit that would drive her to endure, as it had done when Granny Nellie died. Once more, Kelly would push herself to be the best at work, as a housekeeper, and as a mom. She went back to school at night, finishing again at the top of her class. She would be the best, and no one—No one—NO ONE would ever know about her secret horror. More than twelve hundred miles separated her from her past. Kelly had no need for an incentive booster. Being and over-achiever fit her perfectly. She earned the respect of her contemporaries at work and as a single mom. People seemed to assume that Kelly just didn't want to talk about a bad marriage that ended in divorce. And no one ever guessed her dark secret.

On the surface, her world had seemed to come together. She advanced at work. Her children were well mannered, well dressed, in a great school and attending church. Kelly had been drawn to find a fundamental Christian church. She wanted her children to find a part of what she had known in her childhood with granny Nellie. That period of her life provided the framework for how she ran her home. The next few years slipped by. Co-workers would sometimes talk her into a '**girls night out**' or to double with a male friend of theirs. Yet, Kelly never let her guard down. She had no interest in developing a relationship. Her aloof, unattainable air made her a desirable challenge to the few men she went out with. Rarely, she would succumb to unbridled carnal lust and alcohol. Invariably, she would apologize for letting things go too far and refuse to continue a liaison. Her philosophical outlook was jaded. To her mind, love was an overworked and misused word. She loved no one but her children. In the same spectrum of definition, intimacy was nothing more than a transient physical need that quickly faded. It was over so quickly; it was hardly worth the bother. All men ever wanted were sex, a mommy, or a servant. Kelly wasn't even sure why she was attending church, except for her children. The Jesus she believed in, trusted and loved, had betrayed, rejected her. Hadn't he? She lived for her children, to care for and protect them from the atrocities inflicted on her and feeling dirty and vile that never left her.

TIME-OUT

Think Kelly's new life sounds too fantastic to be true? It is very real. While some of the more violent events in her life have been left out, it's important to remember that there is no limit to the cruelty and depravity in the world. Only those with strong moral character adhere to laws and ethics.

Kelly had no way of knowing that her life was like a ticking time bomb, ready to explode at any moment. Women often build emotional walls they believe are unbreakable, but no one is truly an island or an impregnable fortress. There is always a vulnerable spot, usually formed by our deep need for acceptance. No matter how much we try to deny it, this need will eventually break through.

Kelly had been determined to be free of the need for a man in her life. Despite her resolve, she remarried, convinced that her children needed a father. The new marriage was but a few weeks old when she learned of her new spouse's addiction to cocaine. They survived a rocky year. She tried to make it work and encouraged him to seek help, but his addiction nearly wiped her out financially. The first blow he struck sealed the fate of their marriage. In less than two years, it was over.

Kelly saw that she was attracting the kind of men she wanted to avoid. She needed something, but what? She signed up for seminars by Zeigler and L.I.F.E. motivational groups, which reinforced her "I'll be the best" attitude but never reached the real problem. She became almost ruthless in business, with a sign hung on her office wall reading, "Make Money or Make Room." Friends were friends, but business was business. Here again, she had no time for dating; kids and work came first. Her cynical view of life made dating prospects slim and of no importance. She didn't need the hassle.

The thread of Kelly's life was a chain of betrayal, hurt, and despair. There was a pervading emptiness that clutched at her heart, ever since her granny had died. The older woman was the only human she had ever been able to trust, who asked nothing more from her than she wanted to give. The one person she could really say cared for her unconditionally was gone. Kelly wasn't even sure if her own children loved her or just needed her. She longed to sit at her grandmother's feet as she brushed her hair and told stories of her youth to Kelly. There was still a long road to recovery for Kelly.

Not unlike many women who have suffered major trauma, for all her success, something continued to elude her. Something phantom-like, ephemeral, nebulous was drifting in her memory. Especially at Christmas or Easter, Kelly was drawn to church. But when she got there, she only went through the motions of worship. The ache of missing her grandmother and the life of so long ago always surfaced, haunting her. Those holidays had been special events in her early life. Kelly would paste on a smile, shake hands, and say the sermon was 'nice'. Oh, why? Why was she so empty? She had even heard Corrie Ten Boom speak once, but again, she was only half there. Her mind drifted, not attending to all that the old woman shared. Years would pass before she would recall the '**sweet old lady**'. The woman's name didn't stir in her memory until reading some of the old matron's writings. She flipped the book over and looked at the photo on the jacket. A few words floated back now with a stirring of the Texas church she had attended when the woman had spoken there. She regretted an opportunity missed in coming to know someone who had been through a living hell worse than her own.

That ephemeral spirit was tugging at her again. A long road lay ahead before she would get beyond the calloused, fatalistic views she'd adopted. The next card drawn in the deck of life was an auto accident that took several months of recovery. As the time stretched and the bills grew, Kelly worried about her dwindling resources. She learned just how quickly so-called friends had no time for a bedridden woman with two kids. What sounded like an offer sent from heaven came from an associate. He had a house with an extra room. Kelly and her children were welcome until she got stronger. In time, Kelly would learn that there were no silver linings to storm clouds. She was wakened one night by his getting into bed with her. She was physically unable to do anything. Kindness? This is what he wanted for his kindness?

The insurance company wanted to settle with Kelly for the accident. Kelly was having difficulty focusing on anything but getting well. Her '**friend**' would take care of everything if she would marry him. Things were closing in on her: finances, kids who were now pre-teens, and therapy. She was heavily medicated a lot of the time and she couldn't stay focused. Therapy was barely breaching the wall of pain and she married her would-be mentor. Or so she thought. In eight months, she had gotten strong enough to begin handling some of her own affairs, if not walking too well. Shopping was a way of getting her household organized. She asked about money and got vague answers. Checks were being returned NSF. There must be some mistake. She went to the bank. He had taken large sums from the bank account on a regular basis over the last several months. The thirty-five thousand dollars that was left after paying her medical bills, attorney fees, and purchasing a home was gone. Gone in the last three months! For what? She calculated that about twenty thousand went into her new home. That left fifteen thousand. Where was it? What had he done with it? She confronted him. Confrontation bore no fruit. The weeks that followed were filled with arguing. He had quit his job. She discovered more lies. He'd "had his own expenses," he'd said. What expenses? He lived rent-free. Her money paid for the household expenses. He moved in with a woman in a neighboring town. Kelly sought out a lawyer for a divorce. What she learned was that the marriage had been bogus. Bogus! He was a con man! Had someone painted "SUCKER" in bright red paint on her forehead? She would hold her head and move forward. He wasn't the first to rob her in one way or another. Yet, each time she wondered '**why?**' "Why am I always getting into situations?" "Am I so gullible, naïve, or stupid?"

Dead ends or failures rose up at every turn. Casual observers would say she had a lot going for her. She had a roof over her head, no outstanding debts, and a usable car, but she'd have to find a way to make a living. Eventually, she sold her home and moved again. Where would it end? All the moving? The problems? Some of the pieces of the puzzle were missing. What was it? Was she crazy or just weird? Each time she got ahead, someone stripped it away. Was she stupid? That's what the men who had parted from her threw at her. She had started over three, or was it four, times? She had lost thousands of dollars in the process, money that could have given her a comfortable living. But she had lost something else, something priceless. But she did not realize what it was.

TIME-OUT

It has become obvious that a pattern is developing to a reader. But in life, those involved rarely are aware of a pattern, only the number of failed relationships. It is a scene echoed in at least thirty percent of the broken homes in America. Kelly is far from being alone in her dilemma. Cynically, some say, "Who cares?!" To people in Kelly's situation, as in her mind, no one cares about her or what is happening in her life. Kelly, like so many other women, falls into a habit that says, "I'm out here alone." Nobody cares, so something must be wrong with her. All hope is gone. Kelly wanted to die. Depression becomes oppressive, but even suicide is not an option she can pull off. In her situation, a woman will not try to make changes. She has been taught to think she doesn't deserve better. She's been told some part of her is so bad that she is being punished.

At the other end of the spectrum is the perpetual victim, forever bemoaning her lot. "Poor pitiful me." This woman makes no effort to change. To her, it is beyond her ability to do anything but whine.

Optimistically, Kelly began to think the worst was over. The drawing in her spirit led her to find a church. But her walk with God was on and off. Although she was unaware of a change in herself, she was growing spiritually. Kelly had begun to think that what she needed must be a man in her life to make her feel whole, a companion. She had not matured enough in her spirit to turn her need over to God. Nor was she ready to realize the man she was longing for was God himself. A step above taking control of her own life. So she dated. The men were from her work mostly. They all said they knew God. But in retrospect, Kelly would apprehend that if they had a relationship with God, they didn't live it. They didn't actually commit to overcoming their mistakes. They seemed to just follow their urges as always. They were just like every other man Kelly had ever known; driven by lust, having personal addictions to alcohol, drugs, tobacco, or just sex. Kelly's circle of friends began changing slowly. Then, she met a man that she thought more than once was a godsend, Jack O'Shea. In under a year, her rosy dreams were coming apart. Her alleged '**born again**' partner was staying away for days, lying about going to work, and they argued continually. Still, again, she was subjected to the cutting remarks of verbal abuse. He had turned into another person, one she did not know. He was drinking heavily and staying. sometimes, for weeks at a time. He came in reeking of stale beer and sweat. She was accused of trying to mother him, should she attempt to broach the problems and his long absences. He was a '**man**'. He'd make his '**own decisions and go wherever in hell (he) wanted**'. Kelly's nightmare wasn't over.

***

Let's step away from Kelly's story for a moment to look at another woman whose life intertwines with hers. We will call her Kiera, Kelly's older daughter. Now a young mother, Kiera began dating another man soon after breaking up with her baby's father, whom she caught with another woman. The new man, Charles, promised her the moon and swore he would care for her son Joey as his own. However, he soon began pushing Joey severely for trivial mistakes.

Kiera feared the attacks would worsen when she wasn't home but rationalized her fear, believing Joey was acting out because Charles wasn't his father. The relationship became a battleground, filled with absences, lies, and hostility between Charles and Joey. Kiera began to suspect Charles of being unfaithful, especially after contracting an STD, which she tried to believe came from a toilet seat. The OBGYN confirmed it was an STD passed by someone with multiple sex partners.

Kiera, stuck in a cycle of abuse like her mother, had another child with Charles. While he doted on their daughter, he pushed Joey aside, calling him a "little bastard." As years passed, Kiera's hopes of saving the marriage faded. Charles's hostility grew, affecting their daughter, who started crying in her sleep, wetting her pants, and pushing other children. Overwhelmed, Kiera struggled to discipline without anger.

One day, Joey, crying and trembling, told a neighbor, "If he hits me again or hurts my mom, I'll kill him!" At nine years old, Joey had drawn the battle lines. It took courage for Kiera to report Charles to Children's Protective Services. But the cut lip and belt marks on Joey's back were too much. She thanked God it hadn't been worse.

Kiera recalled a news story about a Kentucky senator. He abused his stepson, chaining him to a bathroom commode for months. The boy, eventually escaped. It reminded her of Charles. He would confine Joey to his room, make him run in place for an hour, and do 100 sit-ups to "show him who's boss." Joey, suffering from ADHD, was often denied his medication by Charles, who wanted to break his spirit.

Kiera couldn't believe how much Charles had deceived her. She had never seen him hit Joey; he only yelled and confined him when she was around. She hoped they would adjust, but Joey never liked Charles. Had he seen what she hadn't? Suspicion arose when the school reported a bruise on Joey's face shortly after she married Charles. Charles claimed Joey had tripped over toys, and Joey was frightened by the strangers questioning him. Joey mumbled, "I just fell," under the stress of it all.

The past had led to her abuse and now her children's. She hated what being beaten and seeing her battered had done to her children. Solving conflicts before they reached this point was never taught. It was always about winning an argument, about defeating the spouse. The idea of being better for each other and figuring things out together never occurred. Letting others 'practice with grace' was considered weak instead of displaying strength. It was mostly themselves and their children who stayed in pain as punishment. They hid in fear when 'daddy' was around, lurking about, trying not to be seen. Now, it was Charles. He backhanded Joey and cursed him, calling him a bastard.

Joey was not illegitimate. And what if he was? It was no reason to mistreat a child. Charles' new tangent was that he forbade them to attend church and found other things he could take away, even from Kiera herself. It troubled Kiera. She'd come home from work to hear conflicting stories about what Joey had allegedly done and his latest punishment. But Kiera couldn't protect her son every second. Joey was becoming more defensive and rebellious. He was getting into trouble at school. Their lives had fallen into a routine. When Joey and Charles collided wills, she believed Joey was being rebellious. The antagonism escalated for four years between the three of them. Her daughter was a pawn in the argument of both sides. That was when she received a telephone call at her job from a neighbor about lacerations on the boy's back and a bleeding mouth. That had been the final straw. She had not recovered from the shock of the call when she heard the caller continue, "He's been outside for about two hours." He had been without a coat, hiding until someone he felt safe with had found him. It was forty degrees Fahrenheit! There was also the wind chill from the twenty-mile-an-hour wind. Kiera's choice confronted her. Did she want the caller to phone the police, or would she prefer to do so? It is always hard to do the inevitable in a case like this. She called the police station and headed home. The police had arrived and, with some resistance, taken Charles into custody. Charles looked at Kiera and said, "Why are you doing this to me?" Later in court, he would ask, wasn't a person allowed to correct a kid? Correction and abuse are two very different things.

Returning to Kelly, she would need to get her life back together. She had hidden her grief in public. Alone, especially at night, she wept and prayed for hours. She would ask how she had come to yet another failure. She blamed herself for Kiera's broken life and those of her grandchildren. Not even the beatings had been the end of Charles' abuse of her daughter and her children. He had been exposed for molesting both the children and exposing them to pornography. Tears fell hotly down her face as Kelly poured her heart out to God. Kelly had reached her breaking point. She cried for the years of rejection. She lost her granny Nellie. She felt rejected by Jesus. She suffered rapes and countless abuses. Her children grew up. She feared she had failed them. She cried for all the times she had started over. All the tears that had never fallen before finally spilled out. She would fall asleep weeping and seeking God to awake, still weeping, and begin anew. "God, I am somebody. But I don't know who I am. Forgive me, please, for all my sins, for being unlovable. There are so many. I can't do this anymore. I want to die. But I don't want to die a failure. If I must go on living, I need a reason for living," she prayed. She repeated the process until she was totally spent and fell into a deep sleep. She woke ten hours later, feeling refreshed and strangely light. Outside, birds sang, the sun shone, and the air smelled of the promise of spring flowers. Kelly had begun to heal. Some would suggest that this prayer was enough to get these intrusive thoughts off her chest and let her sleep. But it felt good. She didn't feel alone in the moment. She wouldn't think about the road ahead. She had a lot of junk to get out of her life. It would take more prayer. It would take more talking things through at the end of the day. Facing responsibility for the bad choices in her life would take work. Kelly wouldn't be doing it alone. That prayer, in some way, had altered everything. She would not always like what she learned about herself. There would be a sifting of everything. What were the things she had responsibility for and which were not of her making? It would serve no good purpose to beat herself up any longer. A new door had opened to her. Did she have the courage to close the door on the past, to step through the new door? Guilt-whipping? No more. Confess, repent, and ask for help to change. It sounded like a simple formula, simple, yes. Easy? No. Advisors would say to '**take it one day at a time**'. Realistically, it would be hour to hour. Transition would come. Kelly could not help her children until she helped herself. "I will find a way to break the cycle of pain and abuse," she promised herself. "For my kids and their kids." Previously, she had allowed fear to control her. With her own life, Kelly had begun the work without even realizing it, on the day she had poured out all her hurt and failure to God.

PART 3

Moving Forward

True to her nature, Kelly often saw herself through others' eyes. This time, she compared herself to women of high moral character. As she read her Bible, she tried to measure herself against the great women of Scripture. Abigail risked her life to fix an injustice by her husband. She got a blessing for her whole family. Esther and Ruth, who courageously followed God's will. For Ruth, it had meant stepping into the unknown and leaving grief behind. The Proverbs 31 woman was her ultimate model. Kelly saw many areas in herself that needed improvement. Like Dorcas, she always helped others, and like Lydia, she opened her home in Christian love. With these examples in mind, she assessed herself as not being a total zero. Maybe there was hope for her. Since that time of incessant prayer and weeping, Kelly felt a new buoyancy in her spirit. Armed with her newfound freedom, she believed she could open dark, forbidding doors and discover the woman of great value she truly was.

Healing cannot begin until we face our grief and implement changes in our behavior. For Kelly, these changes included following in her grandmother's footsteps and believing in God. She recognized she could not handle it alone and opened up her life to God through prayer. There is an innate part of the human soul that yearns to turn to a higher place or being that rises up from deep inside. Piece by piece, she began to examine her life.

Reflecting upon her life, Kelly realized she should start from a point where she was most happy. For many, that point is childhood. But beyond that, the first traumatic event she could remember was when she was four years old. Her mommy had been very angry, too angry. She had lashed out at Kelly both verbally and physically. The child had no basis for understanding the anger. One day, Kelly had accidentally been too loud and woken up her baby brother. Kelly's punishment was sitting in the corner of the room, standing there until she figured out what she had done wrong. While her mommy was cooking, she listened to her mutter under her breath. This was common.

Kelly still remembers the wallpaper—a soft, creamy color with tiny flowers and cherries or apples. While she was sitting there, she noticed the wallpaper move. Truthfully, she was drifting asleep in the corner, but how was she to know as a young girl? She thought she saw her dad in the dream, get hurt. Sitting up, she snapped back to reality, everything had changed. She had been so sure her dream was real that she ran to tell her mother, urgently tugging at her dress.

"Mommy, Mommy! I saw Daddy's car, and it looked hurt!" she cried out.

Her mother's eyes, dark and stormy, turned on her with a glare. "Kelly, stop making things up!"

Kelly replayed the dream like a movie reel after that. The memory was sharply etched in her mind: the dress she wore, the wallpaper, and seeing her daddy in an accident. That was what the frantic child had told her mother. She also remembered her mother holding tightly to one arm as she kept hitting her and calling her evil. Her mom didn't think kindly of her "daydream."

Kelly was reaching for something more. She tried, vainly, to remember more about her mother from that period. Nothing else. No memory of hugs. There was routine, an impression of cleanliness, and nothing else. Routine was something that Kelly would come to resent as her childhood slipped by. Each recollection of times spent with her mother was tainted with some thread of strict regimen and angry words. Her mother's houses were always clean, almost sterile, devoid of life. There were no images of toys, laughter, or clutter, only a sense of coldness. Perhaps it was because there was no love in them. She could not make that call. Kelly would recall other things her mother had said, things that hurt.

"He doesn't love us anymore," her mother had once said about her father.

Kelly knew that wasn't true, but the child she had been couldn't understand her mother's own hurt. The ritual went on until Kelly was nearly grown. It was a cycle of living at Granny's, then trips with her mother to fix her marriage, angry words, and her father's voice saying, "Oh, to hell with it." That was the only thing Kelly could identify. It was her father's voice. How she longed for her father's love. She had a fleeting memory of sitting on his lap, held tightly, feeling safe and what?... loved? The smell of outdoors on his clothes. Disjointed memories. The cycle would fade only to be resumed. Then, Mommy would leave too. To her daughter, that meant one thing. If Daddy had gone away because he no longer loved them, then her mother must not love her either. What was wrong with her? Was she so unlovable? Was she evil, as her mother had said? Such thoughts had haunted her childhood. They rose up again and again in her life as an adult. It had been her granny's love and nurturing that had broken through the child's reserve. Her granny's capacity to be with her. And Kelly searched for the same capacity for the rest of her life. That's what made God a cornerstone in Kelly's life, God was always within reach.

Kelly blamed herself for the cycle of pain and abuse. She blamed her own inadequacies, real or otherwise, for all that was wrong in her life. She believed she was inferior to everyone else. They had normal homes and parents who did things with them, gave hugs, and laughed.

Alice Von Hildebrand, PhD, confirms that medicine and psychology now accept that a lack of touch can harm a child. These children often spend their lives searching for a nurturing touch and an embrace that remains unfulfilled. Spoken blessings of love and acceptance are absent from many homes, and without these, children don't learn how to connect with others. This leads to co-dependency, a condition that echoes through generations. Many are doomed to failure because their hunger for connection is never satisfied. Relationships formed under these conditions are usually shallow and sex-based. The touch sought is not the one truly needed. Lust isn't lasting, and victims are always crushed by the failure of each relationship, unable to see why it failed.

The essential element of being with a partner is missing, even though sex remains. Victims have low self-esteem and cling to a fading hope that things will be different next time, believing sex will fix it. They often blame the failure on some elusive flaw within themselves. The process of working through the pain of our past takes time. If we keep reliving our traumas in relationships, it breaks them apart.

Generational trauma comes from not having a strong example of a successful relationship. To break this cycle, we need to work through our own traumas. For instance, Kelly's grandmother demonstrated what it means to be present with someone, creating a strong foundation for future relationships. Over time, this effort can make both partners proud to have found someone who is committed to improving each day.

Working through past pain is crucial. Without addressing generational mistakes, we risk teaching the same behaviors to those we connect with. Healing allows us to form genuine connections based on love and mutual respect, rather than temporary fixes that fail to satisfy our deeper needs. By addressing these core issues, we can build healthier, more fulfilling relationships that stand the test of time.

Children are the greatest victims. A lack of touch and affirmation will cause a child to be emotionally delayed. The parent sees the child as unable to make responsible decisions and further handicaps the child by not allowing them to make any decisions for themselves. Once the victim perceives themselves as ugly, unworthy, and inadequate, they accept the unstable world they live in as normal. Then the perverted cycle starts, repeating in later generations because people fail to see the need for help to fix the problem.

Kelly's self-assessment led her to reflect on her relationship with her mother. While Granny Nellie had nurtured her, her mother had been distant and critical. Kelly wanted to understand why the feelings she had toward her mother were confused. She knew that her granny had become a widow at an early age, with young children to support amid an economic depression. Having to work outside the home caused Kelly's mother and her younger siblings to miss out. They didn't receive the same care and comfort as the older siblings, who had both parents. Any sacrifice made was for survival, not neglect. The nation was in the post-war era of the Great Depression. There was no way to predict which child would rise above the circumstances and which would be emotionally crippled.

What about Kelly's father? Born in the same depression period that had no hold on stability, his parents divorced when he was barely thirteen. He had to strike out on his own. He had no idea where he was going, had neither skills nor a way to make a living. His mother could not provide for both him and his siblings. So, he made sure she had one less mouth to feed. There was no father to guide him into manhood, just the raw exposure to the, often seedier, other side of life. He learned that survival meant hard work. War came again, this time in Korea, and he was there. Returning, he met and married Kelly's mother. Problems arise in every marriage. Theirs was not exempt. He couldn't handle the arguing and retreated into his work. When accusations of infidelity came, he had no skills for coping with the ensuing arguments, and he left. Just as his own father had done, he'd leave and return until more arguments drove him out. The difference was that his father had been cheating on his marriage. Sam's reaction led to even more suspicion and the eventual destruction of both marriage and family.

So, okay, they had some hard blows, but what did it all mean for Kelly?

She had received the surrogate love of her grandmother. But Kelly was left bereft in adolescence, just fifteen. The love Kelly longed for had come only from her grandmother, who was now gone. She was dependent on that love and acceptance and longed to find it from her mother. But it was not forthcoming.

TIME-OUT

Being in this kind of situation leads survivors to therapists, 'shrinks,' and groups. To many therapists, it becomes a time to listen to someone else drone on about their miserable life. And, therapists just ask questions and give no answers. This allows the people to discover there own solutions. The problem is, most therapists aren't helping the person improve. Their usual forte is, "What do you think?" and "What do you want?" How in the world can a person be expected to answer that? We are sitting here because you DON'T know. We want to be happy, happy, and HAPPY! And, are not, not, NOT! Our mind screams in frustration. "I'm being treated like a child! I'm NOT a child! Nor am I stupid!" Far from it, to all appearances we seem to have ourselves together. You may even be successful in business. Yet, underneath, you are burned out, depressed, dissatisfied, and mentally tired. Looking for someone to connect with. You try to sort out your dilemma by logic. None of the equations add up. Something is missing. You are often empty, lonely, even when surrounded by people. You see them; look at them, as though watching robots busy at varied tasks. Here or there, one of them has a look of being happy. Angrily, you think, "How dare they be happy? What have they got that I haven't?" Children playing at life, they are happy and you resent them for it.

When was the last time you remember being happy? "Laughter, it's all madness," you scorn. "Mirth, what good is it?" What good is pride? You were once proud of your achievements. But now you're in a room with someone getting paid for you to stay "connecting" with them.

***

Kelly was to learn that while she wasn't the worst person alive, she could never measure up to anyone in her mother's eyes. The longing to have that approval became her driving force to excel in anything and everything. It had been the accumulation of circumstances that had led to her low self-esteem and co-dependency. Only now, as she assessed the facets of her life, could Kelly identify the problems. Once she learned to recognize why things happened, she could tell which were beyond her control. She also could tell which were her choices that caused her woes. The chief source of her pain was the desire for the affection of her parents. She wanted to be accepted so badly that she had compromised several of her personal goals and values. This was a bad choice, but it is one commonly made by women. One by one, Kelly looked at several bad choices she had made. Giving these to God by repenting and moving on with living, rather than beating herself up, would be important. She made up her mind to take life one day at a time. Inevitably, there would be other failures. But, Kelly determined that she would be resilient. She would take each day for what it was and the things she had to deal with in the context of that day. She would check herself when she began to deride herself as a failure at everything. She was not a failure at everything. She had to remind herself of that often. It would cause her to recall what a pastor had said once. "It doesn't matter how many times you fall; just as long as you get back up." This time, as she started over, she wasn't doing it alone.

None of us are failures at everything. Though imprisoned by fear and depression, it may appear that way. Kelly, as every woman (even you) in her position, would have to refer to her notes to reassure herself that she did have gifts and talents. She would need to develop those gifts, couple them with her new spiritual zeal, and become the creation that God had intended her to be. Not the shadow or image of someone else, she would be Kelly Jones, unique and beautiful.

It is, on occasion, difficult to focus and keep priorities in order. Temptation is strong to take your eyes off the important things and instead look at the immediacy of food, shelter, and clothing. Kelly had let these distract her decisions in the past. Her main goal was to influence her previous decisions. She drew upon another memory now, that of a parable of Jesus about the birds and the lilies of the field. She also knew that scripture promises that our needs would be supplied. She certainly had no possessions to encumber her. Everything was gone: money, property, all of it. Her children were growing up fast, mostly on their own and having children. Suddenly, Kelly knew another area that needed work. Just who was Kelly Jones? Well, she was no longer Tom, Dick, or Harry's wife. Oh, she was, and always would be, mother to Kiers and Aleana, and grandmother to Joey and Karin. Her sense of being needed was diminished. She no longer was so-and-so's boss, or a student earning her Associate or B.A. anymore. She made a list of who she was, NO, what she used to do. She wasn't just Sam and Elizabeth Jones' daughter, or Nellie's granddaughter. She wanted to know who she was. Kelly had pleaded for God's intervention. Did she still believe in Him? Once, she had believed He had rejected her. Was that true? Had she been wrong?

Kelly was feeling more buoyant and alive since her desperate pleas and subsequent studies. If she believed any part of the sacred word, she had to believe it all. Either Jesus was her savior and God was her Father, or it was all a lie. She needed something solid for her family to learn from. She knew the pain of not having a living example of love, so the Bible to over. What was it she had read? "I will never leave you or forsake you." "...My God shall supply all your needs according to His riches and glory by Christ Jesus." She dreaded opening the door that led to what she had believed to be her rejection by God. Her rejection? Had He really rejected her or had she misunderstood and subsequently rejected Him? As she pondered it, she smiled at a small boy who ran past her. His shirt read, "God don't make no junk." No, she supposed not. But, boy, we could sure get way off track. Kelly knew she would have to find the person she was inside. As she began rediscovering herself, she rediscovered her relationship with God. She had made such a mess of her life. She needed to reclaim what she had lost. Not literally tangible things actually.

But, piece by piece, her values and her own ideals. More than anything, she wanted to know WHO Kelly Eagle was. She was not the alcohol, drugs, and tobacco she had tried. "Thank you, God," she prayed, "for saving me from those things and the consequences they could have carried." There could have been much more terrible consequences she could have had to suffer for her choices. She hadn't prostituted. But, she was sometimes promiscuous and careless about protecting herself. She again sought forgiveness and gave solemn thanks for being spared. So many things kept surfacing. With each, Kelly saw how narrowly she had escaped potentially fatal consequences. In each, she knew that someone, or something, had been looking out for her. Someone had once told her she could fall into manure and come up smelling like a rose. It was funny how things kept coming back to her.

That person had been right, of course. She had fallen, or stepped, in a lot of manure. "One thing about manure though, it makes terrific fertilizer," Kelly smiled to herself. "I should burst out in blooms all over." She had said the last part aloud. But, roses, so beautiful, also have thorns. For all the bad choices she had made, Kelly had made at least one right choice. She had accepted Jesus as her Savior and God as Father. She would come to see that choice from a new perspective. A new awareness was emerging that would lead her to baptism. She had been baptized many years before, when she had first accepted salvation. What was it now that she was seeking? What was it called? Rededication?

Yes, but something more. How could she put it into terms that made sense? Salvation was wonderful and knowing she had been forgiven so much. What she wanted to communicate to herself and the world had deeper meaning, and it was very real. She wanted everything and everyone, including God, to know He was not only Savior and God, but also Lord of her life. There was almost euphoria at the thought. "I love you, Lord," she said audibly. "I really love you." She spoke toward the clear, blue sky and laughed. How wonderful she felt. Mary Magdalene must have felt like this when Jesus forgave her past and freed her of what some have labeled a mental disorder. Kelly had been given so much that she had taken for granted. On the other side of practicality, there were still a lot of adjustments to be made in Kelly's life. Life is a school from which we never graduate. Each change, every door opened or closed, was a new adventure, a time of discovery. Scripture said that we can grow up to Him in all things. Did Kelly know herself yet? Not entirely. There was a person she desperately wanted to know. Moving forward with her assessment of her life would be extensive. Still, it didn't have to be a preoccupation. Her spirit now knew the deep craving, thirst, and hunger for more of God in her life. Prayer had become a daily part, and sometimes, an ongoing conversation, in her life.

***

Shifting gears, we can assume a fatalistic reasoning that would say, "You have to pay the fiddler if you're going to dance."

Kelly had to reach this point, striving to move away from stagnant thinking to modify as much as possible for any woman. Like Kelly, you will reach a juncture where you seek to make changes. You must forgive yourself, understand what hairnet and then put something in is place. You may observe the inner woman growing and maturing. Old cronies may mock your new choices but what kind of friends do that? This is especially true if you now attend church and have lost interest in reveling and going to clubs. Don't quit! Keep in mind that '**misery loves company.**' They don't want you to change. You won't be fun to be with if you aren't enslaved to debauchery or decadent self-destruction. What is even worse, in their thinking, is you are making them see the flaws in their own lives. They perceive the changes as threatening. Change means unfamiliar, uncharted vulnerability. You are opening new doors, embarking on your adventure. Both your old pals and the old you will try to convince you it's useless, that you will never be different. You're just putting on airs, trying to be something you're not. Lies! Lies! Lies! It is a hard-fought battle, and you must keep your courage up. You cannot do it any other way. There is one alternative to fighting the battle alone. You can choose, as Kelly did, to place your life in the capable and loving hands of God. You will have work to do. You just no longer have to do so alone. To know where the Lord wills you to be led is in His word. There are some pretty strong guidelines for living in Scripture. It tells us that God knows all things we need but requires us to ask. He desires a relationship with us, His children. He wants our trust and to be first in our lives. To those who love and trust Him, the Bible is a guidebook, an instruction manual for everyday living. A preacher, long ago in Kelly's life, had said the word BIBLE stood for Basic Instruction Before Leaving Earth. It was another of the little things that came up to enrich her journey. Got a problem? Or a question? There is either an illustration bearing the correct way to deal with a situation or a direct command for it. It includes references for family, interaction with others, and even marriage and child-rearing. In our anxiety for a quick answer, we sometimes plead for God's help. A problem arises when, seeing no results, we decide to take matters into our own hands. We think God wants this. Remember, no change happens all at once. To expect a utopian, idealistic life simply by confessing or repenting to be immediate is unrealistic. To be willing to change is to stand at the threshold. Change then comes much like reading a book, turning one page at a time. To skip over pages would cause you to lose the plot or miss the purpose for which it was written. Many high school students have learned that lesson to their dismay. You cannot read the first chapter of the book and the dust jacket or final chapter, and receive a passing grade on a report. There are no shortcuts to a job well done. Life is layer upon layer of experience, choices, and cause and effect. Your life is a tapestry, woven one episode at a time. Each episode is linked to those before and after it. The same is true of changes that occur from reversing the manner of making choices, layer by layer.

Kelly was destined to make mistakes, as we all are. It is a part of life. The most common error, like Kelly, is thinking we won't make mistakes anymore. Similarly, many new Christians assume they will no longer 'screw up.' They think this because they have accepted salvation. In reality, we become like the apostle Paul, who was aware of a warring in his being between the spirit man and the carnal man. That we will, in our own imperfect state, make a wrong choice is a given. The objective lesson is not to beat yourself up over your mistakes. It is key to recognize the mistake, admit it, and rise above it. To wallow in shame or self-pity would, literally, be a fatal mistake. "You shall be holy because I am holy," states the gospel. What is holy? What does it mean to live a holy lifestyle? It is not merely professing a religion. Many attend church because their mother, father, or grandparents did. True faith and religion must be a way of life, not merely a practice. Those who make a religion a practice have lives no different from those of non-believers apart from their churches. How can you know what it means to be holy? If you knew you were dying, how would you prepare for your last week? Would you live like hell, trying to do all that you could never do before? Or would you take the time to reflect on your life? You would see if anything would keep you out of heaven. This is especially true if you aren't sure if there is a God or heaven. Just in case He and heaven are real, what would you do? Would you begin seeking the face of God in prayer and repentance? Would you turn to sacred writings about what His plan for mankind is?

Some of the synonyms for holiness are sanctified, sacred, pious, godly, virtuous, and saintly. If some words are unfamiliar, a good dictionary can help.

PART 4

Practical Application /
Making a Difference

Making a difference happens one person at a time. No change can bring new life to ourselves or our children until we first change what we do everyday. To keep the application simple, do not look at our situation as a whole but at each part of the problem individually. It can be compared to cleaning a cluttered house. You may look at it in dismay, realizing it will take more time and energy than you have to clean it. But if you focus on one area, say one chair or table, and tell yourself, "I'll start here and do what I can," you are committed to that one project. It's about working on it, rather than completing it all at once. Having completed that task, you can move on to the next, feeling good about your accomplishment.

What is one small area of your life that feels overwhelming? How can you break it down into manageable tasks to start making progress today?

What area of your life needs improvement? Choose something to focus on this week and make a list of small, actionable tasks you can complete to make progress.

Working on Ourselves First

Have you ever looked into your closet and thought, "I really need to get rid of some of the things in here"? You didn't throw out everything, just what you no longer used, right? Our prototype, Kelly, must deal with one choice or issue and the application of the material to it, at a time, as do we. We cannot make changes for our children unless we make changes first for ourselves. Our children often do listen but instead mirror ourselves. This is because before they could speak, they often learned to observe actions first. It isn't selfish to work on us first. If we jump into changes for the kids before working on ourselves, they will likely see it as hypocrisy or our being mean. Telling them to do something we don't ourselves.

As a parent, we could turn to a book called Proverbs as a model for instruction. The text repeatedly expresses a parent speaking to his/her child, "My son, hear the instruction of your Father." Chapter four begins, "My children, hear..." Instruction covers such topics as foolishness, wisdom, knowledge, correction, and countless pearls of truth as recounted in Chapter 22, "A good name is to be chosen rather than great riches..." Proverbs 27 warns that how one thinks in his/her heart is what he/she is. Both in instruction and personal application, we are cautioned about many things apart from carnal/exotic lusts to be wary of. Envy, jealousy, egotism, pride, and low self-esteem have hidden dangers. They bring the risks of anxiety, depression, and loss of zeal. Nearing its close, the book of Proverbs further cautions concerning greed, foolishness, adultery, hateful attitudes, and slothfulness.

Chapter 31, beginning in verse 10, is directed to or about women. It speaks to those who would aspire to high goals in their life and for their family. Though set in the life of a married woman, a single woman can also aspire to high goals. She can do more good spiritually because she is free of the duties of family life. How like a modern woman, who is a wife and/or mother, but also a prudent businesswoman. To attain her goals, the woman doesn't usurp her husband's headship in the home. Nor did she take on a feminist attitude of man-bashing/trashing to feel equal to or better than him. There is no battle for equality. Both have strengths and weaknesses. There is no need to point out the weaknesses of the other. They are a compliment to each other, without holding up individual achievements as to gloat or hold them over the other. Recognizing the uniqueness of the other person does not feel threatening or as a block to the success of the other. In this model, one does not define the other person. Each, being uniquely individual, is not a carbon copy of the other and uses the gifts/talents that God has equipped them with. In a man/woman relationship, as the maker of man created it to be, there is no demeaning of either. Rather, there is to be rejoicing as the union is blessed and is growing together. The Proverbs woman owned property. She sold goods and supervised workers. Her family was well clothed and fed. Her husband praised her to his peers. Her success was no threat to his own.

Parenting with Wisdom

Another place for sound advice is in the letter the apostle Paul wrote to the church at Ephesus. Throughout, there is encouragement to walk worthily of God. Chapter 5 admonishes the reader to be imitators of

God and continues with advice for correct conduct. Chapter 6 begins with advice for children to honor their fathers and mothers. Verse four of that chapter then shifts to the fathers, but in single mom homes it would apply as well. In a two-parent home, fathers have been instructed to enforce discipline. Kelly's mom could have benefited from the admonition, "...do not provoke your child to wrath, but bring them up in the training and admonition of the Lord." Many modern parents face discipline problems because they do not teach Godly habits. Nor do they give direction to their children but seem to expect them to absorb what they are to do by osmosis. When children fail to 'perform', the parent strikes out at, yells, and berates the child for unsatisfactory behavior. The child is confused. No one has told them to do differently. They grow bitter with each attack and often come to resent the parent. Provoked to wrath, they rebel, some killing their parents or contemporaries.

Although given Godly direction to not "spare the rod," it is not a carte blanche invitation to render physical abuse to their children. Corporal punishment is an extreme form of punishment and should be reserved for the correction of extreme forms of misconduct. Punishment and correction should be suitable to the offense. Apart from parenting, scripture counsels both spouses in their duties. It does not focus on their "rights" as chauvinists or feminists. Who better to guide marriage than its inventor? The first man recognized immediately the union to be as "one flesh," two equal parts of a whole. Today, more than 50% of marriages end in divorce. No one should be surprised that even 3,000 years ago the subject of divorce came up. Not with the first pair, but by the time of Moses' writings, it had become necessary to address the problem in the Mosaic law. Later, in the first century of the Common Era, Jesus was asked to clarify the matter. Mark 10:5-12 reads, "Because of the hardness of your hearts he (Moses) wrote you this precept. But, from the beginning of creation, God made them male and female. For this reason, a man shall leave his family and his mother. He will be joined to his wife, and the two will become one flesh. So, they are no longer two but one flesh. Therefore, what God has joined together, let no man separate." He continued, "... Whosoever divorces his wife and marries another commits adultery against her. And, if a woman divorces her husband and marries another, she commits adultery."

Moving Forward

Is there further beneficial material for inter-human relationships? Most certainly. There is a freedom for a person whose partner commits adultery, in that they are free to remarry, just as when a mate has died. The laws set down by Moses and later by the first-century followers of Jesus are long instructions. They tell people to care for the elderly, the homeless, the stranger, the handicapped, and the orphaned. The instruction by Moses is called the "Judaic Law" or "Torah". The first century...

Remember, the journey to personal growth and making a difference starts with a single step. Embrace the process, celebrate your progress, and know that every small change brings you closer to a more fulfilling life. Together, we can create a ripple effect of positive change in our lives and the lives of those around us.

Your story doesn't end here; it's just beginning. Each day offers a chance to grow and inspire others with your courage. Reflect on how far you've come and imagine the possibilities ahead.

Join our community on TikTok @RianMileti to share your journey. Follow for tips, inspiration, and updates on upcoming projects. Check out my other books for more insights and guidance.

Keep moving forward, and remember, the best is yet to come.

THANK YOU
FOR BEING APART OF OUR JOURNEY

Thank you for reading *Inside The Pain*. Whether these stories resonated deeply with you or offered a new perspective, your thoughts mean everything to me.

If you found comfort or insight in these pages, please share it with others and leave a review on Amazon and Goodreads. Your feedback is vital in spreading its message of hope and healing.

Join me on TikTok, where I can't wait to thank you personally. After 20 years and reclaiming my work despite Parkinson's, these stories are alive again because of incredible friends like you.

Your comments inspire me, and I hope my words have touched your heart.

Thank you for being a part of this journey. Together, we can create a future filled with hope and resilience. With heartfelt gratitude,

http://www.RianMileti.com

References/Footnotes

Bible Verses:

- Genesis 1:27; 3:16
- Exodus 6:7; 20:5
- Deuteronomy 6:5
- Job 2:9; 15-23
- Psalms 91:2; 127:3; 146:9; 86:15
- Proverbs 1; 5; 14; 29; 31:10-31
- Ecclesiastes 1:9
- Isaiah 40:8
- Jeremiah 29:11
- Joel 2:13
- Habakkuk 3:21
- Zephaniah 3:1,22
- 2 Peter 3:18
- 1 John 1:8
- Revelation 21:4
- Hebrews 5:20; 6:18; 11:1; 13:4-5
- James 1:5-8; 4:1,42

- Matthew 5:33,44-45;
- Mark 12:30-31
- Luke 15:11-31
- John 3:16; 8:32; 10:10
- Acts 9:36-41; 16:14,40; 17:11
- Romans 3:4; 6:23; 7:17-24; 8:28; 9:15
- 1 Corinthians 6:14; 7; 12:7; 13:4-7
- 2 Corinthians 7:14
- Galatians 5
- Ephesians 2:5,19-22; 4:15; 5:25-29
- Philippians 4:13,19
- Colossians 3:17,19
- 1 Timothy 3:16
- 2 Timothy 1:7-12
- 1 Peter 2:9-10; 3

Books:

- The Real Bottom Line, Dr. Bernie Seagal

Interviews:

- St. John's Seminary interview, EWTN 8-05-00

Summary

"Inside the Pain" delves into the impact of modern pressures and media on families, offering advice for healthier relationships. It provides victims with clear steps to break the cycle of abuse, emphasizing support, boundaries, and self-worth through personal stories. The book addresses childhood issues and substance abuse, refusing to excuse ongoing problems. It advocates for the chance to reshape learned behaviors, promoting balanced, loving parenting over strict, cold homes. The widespread issue of broken trust in families, counselling, clergy, and politics is also discussed.

"Inside the Pain" presents a plan for victims to rebuild their lives free from abuse, guiding readers towards a better future and empowering them to create change in their lives and communities. These tools can help end the cycle of violence and build a society where trust, love, and healthy relationships thrive.

Made in the USA
Middletown, DE
03 September 2024